Toby

a play by
Russell Gregory

Toby

a play

by Russell Gregory

ISBN 13:   XXX-XXX-XXXX

Cover elements, Canva.
Interior design by Lori Graham (Pocahontas Press).

POCAHONTAS PRESS

Floyd , VA
pocahontaspress.com

Dedication

I dedicate this play to John Lawrence Gregory, my
cousin who was also my true brother; he suffered
and celebrated along with me until his death. We
both knew Toby and wished him well. At the same
time I thank Katy Caussin and the original cast who
brought *Toby* to life.

Cast of Characters

Toby Barrister (TB) Male -

Toby is a person who thought everything in life was supposed to fit with the least amount of adjustment. In his mind, you grow up, are protected, go to school, college, train for a job and marry your life-long spouse, get a job, have a family, meet all your obligations, then die with dignity, peacefully, after a long and distinguished career. For really minor reasons Toby derailed and continued crashing. He lives a lie and works in an unskilled position that barely allows him to get by. He is twenty-nine, well-educated but naïve and frustrated. He is nice but his anger and sense of reality need to catch up. He is wearing his work clothes—jeans and a work-short sleeve shirt which are both covered with signs of his job, for example, flour.

"Mom" (M) Female -

She is in her late 50's and fervently protective, or, over-protective. Though normally submissive to the male figures, especially D, she has strong ideas and fights for them directly and by suggestion. She wears a conservative dress which is not in any way prudish, but very feminine, I.e., complimentary to her figure.

"Dad" (D) Male -

Dad is also in his late 50's. He is not particularly emotional in this struggle. He has principles and those must not be compromised. When "his son" begins to slip away, he does not implore him to stay, out of attachment, but almost commands him not to commit suicide because it is not right (Hegelian—the categorical imperative). He is abrupt and "right". He wears a suit but he will take off the coat as problems arise. He will never loosen his tie.

"Counselor" (C) Male –

Here is a character modeled on THE SATAN we find in the biblical book of JOB. He is not the devil: he is not a tempter in a devilish sense. He is merely the person who seems to have a sixth sense, but knows what is really on Toby's mind most of the time. Or, this is the part of us which we discover normally after we have done something and figured out why we (apparently) acted in such a way. He dresses casually, but professionally. He roams the stage the whole play as though he were a lawyer involved in closing arguments which sums up the whole case.

"Childhood Friend" (CF) Male –

He reflects the young friend of Toby—not particularly good looking but a wonderful person. Affable and caring, he is there to help. He is dressed casually, perhaps in shorts, with a bit of mismatching. In the Radford presentation, the director determined to have this character act as though he were thirteen years old, even when he expressed rather sophisticated ideas.

"Woman in her 30's/40's" (30W) Female –

She is primarily a professional woman sharply dressed. She wears a straight skirt with buttons running the whole length but unbuttoned to above the knee, a top which previews (but not brashly exhibits) her bosom unless she leans over at which time the bosom is nicely exposed. She is distant for the most part, uninvolved, but as she realizes that she is affected, she plunges into the fray passionately.

"Bully" (B) Male -

What's there to say? This is a bully. If he is short, he juts his chest out like a bullfrog. If he is tall, he looks down on everyone. He is blustery, abrupt and meanspirited. He wears slacks (he's no bum), a bright sports shirt unbuttoned to show his chest hair and gold chain. He does not have a beard; his hair is combed back.

"Iconoclast" (I) Male -

In a sense, "I" is the pushy compliment of "C". "I" always remains on the fringe of society, always pushes the rules, mores, structural principles of groups. He/she supports radical individualism and the complete freedom of choice. At the least, anything goes; at the most, anything and everything goes. She/he dresses at odds with everyone, perhaps like a punker.

"Lost Love" (LL) Female -

She is both what is frustrating about youth and young love—so naïve, sentimental (the sentimentality of the untested), and idealistic or hopeful—the unsullied affection so free from deceit, disappointment, and despair. She dresses fashionably for a young person, and innocently. Whereas 30W wears what she wears because it is fashionable and it looks good on her, 30W also knows the effect clothes have. This young woman, late teenager at the most, dresses without the true understanding of what she does (or can do) to others by means of her clothing. Yet, her strength and the magic of her innocence remains her prime characteristic. She is Eve before the appropriation of the fruit of the tree of the knowledge of good and evil—vulnerable but magnificently strong.

Postman (PM)-

He is a hard-working man who does his job and does not have much to say. A truly marvelous bit part.

Toby was first performed in the Radford University Studio Theatre, November 2-4, 1990. Its cast and crew included:

Katie Caussin, Director
Monte Haught, Assistant Director
Stephanie Will Turner, Stage Manager
Elliot Kahn, Lighting/set design

Todd Charles, Toby Barrister
Robert Burns, Counselor
A.W. Saunders, Dad
Tracie Ruggiero, Mom
Jason Bold, Bully
Jennifer Clayton, Iconoclast
Angela Leigh Murphy, Woman
Dianna Keiler, Lost Love
Bep, Grandma
Jeff Clemmons, Childhood Friend

THE FIVE MOVEMENTS:

I.   Revelation
II. Argument over suicide
III. Bath and fantasy
IV. Decision and interruption
V.   Conclusion

Toby

a play

by Russell Gregory

Staging:

(Toby, wearing a jacket, enters stage carrying a
bag of groceries, a small brown sack with its opening twisted around like a liquor purchase, a
"Duncan donut bag with product, a newspaper, and
some mail. All other actors/actresses are spread
throughout the audience—perhaps rather near the
stage (within the first three rows, with "C" next
to the stage) so they can get onstage reason-
ably quickly. They need to enter the theater with
the other patrons and play their parts even while
waiting to come in. they will literally come out
of the woodwork. Toby puts the groceries on the
counter then crosses to the coffee table. There he
drops one package with a thud, bends down and let's
go of the paper and the mail (it spreads or scat-
ters on the table and floor), and walks back to the
counter.)

                 ****

C: What's that?

TB: (turns his head toward the sound)Huh? What?
(stops for a moment)

C: (still seated)I said: "What's that?"

TB: Well, that over there is my mail and the
newspaper, this is a bag of donuts that my boss
(sarcastically) graciously let me bring home for
breakfast (places them on the counter, and (opening
the refrigerator and placing the objects in as he
speaks) this is milk, (back to the counter) this is
bread, and this is peanut butter.(He takes off his
jacket and hangs it on a hook.)

C: (still sitting) No, what is that(pointing at the
other bag on the coffee table)? Why d'ya get that?

TB: That's all I need, another hassle this morning.

C: I'm just asking a simple question.

TB: (continuing) My boss hassled me all morning because for the last several days I've put the doughnut holes in a little crooked (sarcastically). He claims that nobody likes an unbalanced doughnut. So I made fun of him. He got so mad that he almost fired me. And there (points to a letter) on the floor is a letter from my brother. He wants, I bet(runs over and grabs the letter, holds it to his forehead for a moment then rips it open), yeah, he wants his money back, the money I borrowed a couple of years ago to tide me over. Ha! I needed that money just to survive. I can't pay it back of course, I need more money. My parents want to come see me and if they do, I'm dead. They'll see where I live, what I really do, what I've really become (growing more and more panicked).

C: (feigning interest) So, it's been a rough day. Why that (pointing at the small bag on the coffee table)?

TB: (acknowledging the other package) It's protection; I needed protection. I feel like I'm being watched.(Short nervous pause.) I needed something to make me feel safer, more in control if anything started to happen.

C: (skeptically or sarcastically) Is that right?

TB: It's a reasonable response. (Toby turns and goes to the refrigerator and opens the door, then shuts it. C continues to watch TB.) Besides, why does there always have to be an explanation for everything? (Slams the door and moves to the couch)

D: (Standing as he speaks) Because there always is. (Toby shutters with his body.)

M: (Sitting next to D.) That's right. (Toby sits on the couch. He places his head in his hands.) And it is important that we learn that explanation.

D: That's right. (D helps M to the stage.)

TB: (mockingly) Because there always is. Good God, can't some things just remain a mystery?

B: (On the opposite side from the parents, he slouches in his chair and does not get up as he speaks. He cuts in right after TB.) BECAUSE somebody always knows, (emphatically) I certainly know that's true, (short pause then slowly) somebody always knows.

C: (standing and looking around) Listen. We do not need to argue(firmly). We can stay calm. There is an explanation for your buying that.., that… Well, we do not really know what it is? What is it, Toby? Tell us what it is (slight pause). Tell yourself.

TB: Its protection.

C: Protection is abstract. That is not abstract.

D: (impatient, moving toward TB, and gently pushing M) What do you mean, protection?

M: You can tell us, honey.

TB: Quit pushing me!

B: (still sitting) Quit wasting time. What is it?

D: (both curious and firm) What's so hard about telling us. I mean, what could be so bad that….

TB: (explosively) It's a gun, it's a big gun. It's a 44 magnum. (B gets up and moves on stage as though to take a look. Takes a frustrated breath

and expels it with disgust—he seems both offend-
ed and surprised at the big deal being made out of
this purchase). People go out every day and buy
guns. I'm not the only person who feels like the
world is going to hell. I got a right to buy some
sort of protection. You make me feel like I'm a
criminal.

I: (directly, [from the audience]) Nobody said
that.

M: (surprised by the voice, looks around but does
not find the source and before she does she speaks)
Nobody meant to get you upset.

D: (firmly) We're just trying to get an expla...(M interrupts).

M: We're just concerned.

TB: Okay, okay. (begins an explanation which
should quiet the voices)
I read the paper this morning and the headlines
were a little scary.
(He gets up and paces back and forth as though he
were dramatizing the account, but he does not
really act it out. A guy in the next building,
looks at the rest of the characters slowly move
to the stage, except "I" and "LL", he is trying
to convince any and all of the others) was killed
during a robbery.
(He has the air of a news reporter.)
They caught the perpetrators during the act. (Back
to his account.)
The cops were making a regular pass and they saw
these gang members stabbing this guy. The cops
got 'em, but the guy died twitching and bleeding on
the sidewalk. If that guy would have had a gun, he
would have killed them. He was walking home from
work; (underscore) he had a job. They were scum
(with a note of exasperation). The cops recovered
fifty-eight cents from the assholes. That's all he

had on him. But now he's dead. (pauses) I don't
want to be dead.

C: So, why did you buy the gun?

TB: (just short of a shout) I just told you.

C: You told us why he should have had a gun, but is
that really your reason?

TB: Why shouldn't it be?

C:. You keep asking questions instead of giving
answers. I don't think you want to answer the
questions.

I: (half playfully, half seriously—standing) Perhaps, you ought to try another line of question-
ing, Counselor (moves to the stage and sits on the
edge).

TB: Counselor? More like a prosecutor! I don't
want to submit, I will not submit to a barrage of
voices asking me questions or suggesting what my
motives are or…

C: (sarcasm mixed with faux concern) Okay, okay,
relax. I forgot. You've just come home from work.
You have not had time to relax yet, have you?
We've, (pause) I've, upset your routine. Excuse
my rudeness. (C backs away; M and D move to him
and get him to sit on the couch. D stands by the
couch; M sits by TB. 30W stands and looks at what
is going on with interest.)

M: (after a short pause, she speaks) How was your
day? (Toby stretches out with his head on the back
of the couch.) That job tires you too much. It's
just not right for you.

D: You need a better job, one that gives you a
sense of satisfaction.

TB: I was promised a rest. (30W glides to back of the couch and looks down at TB.) I don't want to be bothered again for a few minutes at least. I just want to lie here and let my mind go.

30W: (leaning over so that her breasts almost touch his face, a salacious voice) We, I, can help you.

TB: (Turning his head to see who is speaking only to gaze right down her blouse.) I don't think so.

30W: (She smiles and slowly stands) Why not?

TB: (turning back as his focus leaves her and he looks back at the others) Because when you say you are going to help me, that generally means you are going to question me and you release a whole Pandora's box of questions. Then the clamor begins again and I can't get unwound. I don't need help; I need to be completely alone.

30W: (ss she moves around toward the others, then continuing to tease) Nobody wants to be alone.

TB: How do you know? (Scanning them all as he paus-es—then confidently as he stands.) You don't. How could you know? You've never been alone. I'd like to be rid of you, I'd like to be rid of this place (waves arm), I'd like to be rid of my job, to be rid of the whole damn world.

C: (moves toward TB) But how could you do that, or, (with an investigative tone) how are you going to do that? You really can't get rid of the whole "damn world" (highlights his quote from TB) so how are you going to get alone?

TB: (Defensively, realizing that he was the one who opened that Pandora's box. Sits down as he speaks, puts his elbows on his knees but let's his hands hang forward, and looks down as he finishes his line.) I was promised some rest.

C: Have you ever noticed that what you call rest is called escape by everyone else?

TB: (looks up and shouts) **Rest!!**

D: (looking at his watch) You know you really can't rest too long. You need to eat breakfast. Or, if you're so tired from working all night you need to sleep.

TB: No, I just need to rest.

D: No, no, no(authoritatively). Sleep would be better.

TB: (slowly) I want to rest. I know I can sleep. I know I can close my eyes and drift off when I'm tired. But I can never rest. (looking around) Rest means to have none of these voices. Rest means having an empty mind. No words, no thoughts. I'm tired of thoughts, words, voices, of struggle (leans back on the couch).

M: Maybe we, (looking at C) or some of us, have troubled you.

B: Don't baby him. He must face reality; he must face us.

C: Exactly.

TB: (frustrated and cross so that he almost hisses) Rest.

30W: I guess I don't understand the importance of your rest. Why do you want silence?

TB: (Sees a chance to speak to all while addressing this one's question.) Okay. I'll go over this one more time. Then, I want silence.

M: Certainly.

D: Of course.

B: Sure

I: (still in audience) If that is what you want.

C: (with obvious sarcasm as he bows) Whatever you want.

30W: Where do we start?

(During the last exchange, LL has moved on to the stage and eased upstage against the back wall. She will come forward when she speaks.)

TB: (taking charge, standing) We start with me and my life.

LL: This may be helpful, to hear about his life (she comes on stage as far as downstage as possible).

TB: Right. My life (pause—a long breath, then with new strength). My way.

30W: Wait a minute. I thought you were going to tell me why you want silence.

TB: I am, in my way. I mean to set all of you straight one final time. And to do that, I have to make you see through my eyes. It has got to be my way, understand?
(30W nods assent and looks around. Others are nodding, C,B and I are not.)

D: Well, get on with it.

M: Be patient: let him tell it at his own pace.

TB: (Pensively, searching for a place to begin—seemingly in charge now.) My life.

B: C'mon. Hurry up.

TB: (Almost like he's been transported away, but more like the exhilaration of being in charge—as long as he is speaking, no one else is.) It's the silliest thing. One of the earliest memories I have is of a gorilla coming down the hall of my house after me.

D: (sharply) This doesn't begin right. Your personal history should include others. It should start with your ancestors, like your grand-parents, your parents, and then you move to your life. You've just started with a memory, not the facts.

TB: (emphatically) That is my history, my memories strung together.

C: (somewhat resolved to this diversion) Let him get on with his story.

TB: Well, this gorilla.

D: Your parents never let a gorilla in the house. This was a dream, wasn't it?

TB: No, no, there was never one in the house (stretches the word) r-e-a-l-l-y. But one time I was sitting on the toilet. Now, the toilet was right by the door which led to a long hall. I glanced quickly (acts it out, sits on the edge of the couch and looks to his left) and saw a gorilla coming down the hall towards me. I was pretty scared. When I looked again, he had vanished.

C: Was that the first time you considered getting a Smith and Wesson 38?

TB: Cut it out! Can't you get that gun out of your mind for a while? (as an aside) I will tell what I

want to tell and I wanted to tell about the
gorilla.

C: Fine, fine. I just ask for a little direction in
your story (demonstratively). You know, the point?
Can you at least hint at the theme to your recol-
lection (slowly spinning around and pointing up).
Perhaps, strange animals I have hallucinated about?
Or toilet musings for the enlightened mind? Or is a
theme or direction part of the problem?

TB: Wait just a minute. (increasingly agitated)
I've just started. I don't tell you the point; you
will discover the point.

C: (A hint of sarcasm) I'm sorry. I get the point.
Anyway, perhaps that is part of your intention, to
illustrate the lack of direction in your life. Is
that right? Am I on the right track? Am I following
you?

TB: (defensively and moving around coffee table)
Earlier you accused me of being so full of
questions. You sure have a load of them. Except you
punctuate your questions with sarcasm and follow
them up with premature judgments, like why I bought
that gun. I'm trying to...

C: I know. (His sarcasm shows—he is face-to-face
with TB.) Give us an acceptable, (with emphasis),
a believable explanation. Isn't that what you are
trying to do?

I: Hey! Let the guy tell his story!

TB: (backs away, looks at 30W) I don't know why I
started there, why that memory sticks with me. I
know (firmly) my history began before that gorilla
came after me. There was the time before that when
my mother told me she came in and I was totally
unresponsive for some reason. I didn't eat or drink
anything. I just laid there.

M: That's right, I remember that.

C: (smiles) Maybe you were thinking about buying a Smith and Wesson 38.

TB: Why are you always so sarcastic? There was a reason for her concern! (He regains his composure.) She had lived through the polio epidemic. She took me to the doctor and he couldn't find anything wrong with me. The next day I was fine. I don't know what was going on because I don't really remember that happening. I've manufactured a bunch of explana-tions but I can never decide which of them is right because I can't remember being inside of that baby. (Looks at D) That's why I don't like history that much; history is told from the outside.

CF: (CF moves closer to TB. He puts his arm around TB's shoulders like a buddy.) Great. We want your story, the one you want to tell. We want your explan…, uh, your, uh, uh, story.

TB: (TB begins to walk back and forth, stroking his hair. He looks at the gathered characters one at a time. He stops and let his head fall backwards so that it rests on his upper back. He rolls his head from side to side and finally let's his head slip over his shoulder so that it hangs forward. All the while small grunts of pleasure and pain escape him and he looks nervously back and forth at all the people. Finally, he looks up as though he sees something.)

B: For crying out loud! Do we have to wait all day?

TB: Quit interrupting.

B: (frustrated) Interrupting what? Speed it up, would ya?

CF: Hold it. (He looks first at B, then at TB.) Take your time, (with a nervous laugh as he looks back

at B), but not too much time (moves back towards
the edge of the stage).

TB: (looks as though he is buying time) I guess because I really enjoyed kindergarten. I remember a
lot about it, like my real life started then. That
was the year that I told the little pink-haired
girl...

30W: Pink-haired girl?

TB: (spins to look at her) Yeah, I don't know where
that came from. I went to high school with her and
she was a blonde. But in kindergarten, she had pink
hair.(then back around to tell his story). Anyway,
I told the pink-haired girl that I didn't like her
anymore. She started crying and ran to the teacher who made me apologize. She made me apologize!
How can you apologize for what you truly feel? But
she told me I had to and sent us to the cloakroom.
So, I went back into the cloakroom with this pink-
haired girl and said: "I don't really mean this and
I still don't like you, but I'm sorry I said what
I said. Somehow she seemed satisfied and went back
into the classroom. That was that.

C: (almost warm and certainly direct) Well, in both
cases you said what you really felt. Maybe she
appreciated the directness (almost affectionately).
You know, Toby, saying what you think and feel, no
matter how harsh, how frightening, you think it is,
works out the best.

TB: (blocking the affection of C) That was also the
year I was in the hospital; I had an
appendectomy.

B: (hands to his head) Get ready. (slinging his
hands out) He'll show us his stitches, have us
count them, then have us feel them, then…

I: (getting up) Hell, let's see his stitche,

(roaming to another place to get a better view).
That'll make his story real, at least more inter-
esting.

TB: (timid as though the comments are beginning to
weigh him down) I don't remember much. I had a
fever and I was vomiting the whole night (acting it
out in broad strokes). Early the next morning, my
parents met the doctor in his office where he looked
in my throat and pulled on rubber gloves and thrust
his hand, it seems to me, though it was probably
one or two fingers up my asshole. I guess he found
something because he told my parents to get me to
the hospital for tests. I remember I had to pee in
a milk jar. The next day they opened and closed me.
I awoke and saw a mound of bandages on my abdomen.
I asked my mother why I was bandaged. She carefully
lifted the edge of the gauze to show me a field of
black stitches and cut skin.

B: (turning his back to TB) Here come the
stitches…

TB: (loudly, cutting back in) I thought those
stitches were pretty amazing (using hand motions
to imitate a sewing machine). I could just imagine some big sewing machine stitching me up. When
I think about that operation now I keep thinking I
could have died—from the disease, from the operation, the gas that put me to sleep, you know, from
hidden complications, from something.

C: Yeah, like a gun hidden in a paper bag.

TB: Stop it, (with an edge in his voice which
judges C for not being able to move on). Can't you
forget about that gun. I'm starting to feel
better now. I don't need your sarcasm.

C: Good enough. (roughly direct) Let's talk
straight about that gun.

TB: I'd rather continue. I have told only part of the story that needs to be told.

C: Not time yet, huh? (Then to himself) Not yet time, (turns and distances himself from TB. Finds the chair, moves through the others, excuses himself several times, and sits down.)

TB: Of course, I didn't die (glancing at the gun, he is a little nervous), but what sticks in my mind is that I wasn't afraid to die. I mean, I didn't even know death existed (half laughs). Sure, I knew people died, but you don't really know death is real until it touches you, until you are involved, until you have to deal with it. What's more, if I would have died, I wouldn't have been mad about it.

I: That's stupid. What do you mean by that?

30W: I think he's right. I mean, what's the point?

M: (interrupts, reflectively, stands) Others would have been sad.

D: You would never have grown up, never reached your potential.

TB: (with a laugh) Yeah. (more realistically) You're all missing the point. If I had surgery now, I would be scared. And if I died, if I died, I would be so angry with whoever screwed up. (angrily) I would be so mad.

I: Dead people don't get mad; they don't hold a grudge. That's crazy.

30W: What is the point?

C: (rapidly, or right after 30W) Or is the point that there is no point?

TB: The point, or **the explanation** as you would call

it (looks at C, 30W, and then D), is that my world now is not shielded by a naïve, childish ignorance. My world is a more fearful place. (Acts as though a discovery has been made.) Maybe that's why the gun is so important to me, yeah, important.

D: Do you think that the world has really changed that much? Isn't it you that has changed, Toby?

TB: (sharply said as he quickly turns toward him) What's the difference? The world I grew up in is gone and that scares me.

B: I don't know how all this talk and all this storytelling is going to get us anywhere. We have a guy who likes to hear himself talk and tell old memories. This is going to go on and on and on and on and…

C: (cutting in as he stands to make his point) No, I think we're beginning to get somewhere (stands up and moves toward TB). I don't think he is running on; he is either running to or from or both.

TB: (somewhat on guard and sarcastic) Since when did you become a therapist?

C: Why the anger? I am not your antagonist; I'm on your side. (Pats TB on the back while looking at TB's face.) I'm trying to help you. You may not believe that, but it's true. Go back to your story…or stories (walks back to his chair, waving his hand to signal TB to continue and sits back down).

TB: All of a sudden I am really tired. I think I need to sleep (moves back to the couch or sofa and lays down. M helps him get comfortable.)

M: You have worked all night. You must be tired.

D: You get so tired because that job is below you—a baker's helper (like he's moving through a list).

I bet it is monotonous. It's also manual labor. You're not trained for it(pause—gestures at TB). You're not built for it. You could be doing a lot less work for a lot more money, something that uses that marvelous head of your's—your brains not your brawn!

M: This is not time to discuss this. Go to sleep.

B: (moving quickly to the couch) Wait a minute. He's got an obligation; he's got to finish what he started. He can't keep jumping around like he's dodging something (pulls TB up by the neck of his shirt and looks around). I'm not going to let this guy go to sleep unless I know what's going on. And he promised to tell his story (emphasized) and apparently in great detail.

30W: (moving behind the couch and breaking the grip on TB) Why don't we let him rest and (winking at him) then he will be stronger.

D: A nap never hurt anyone.

B: (pointing) He's the one who showed so much urgency. Now, he wants to sleep. I think we ought to hold him to at least one course of action. He's so indecisive. If he can't discipline himself, we'll do it for him.

M: (pushing TB down) But he's dog-tired. He can't think!

B: (punching TB in the chest with his index finger) Hey, remember—when the going gets tough, the tough gets going.

TB: (Shouts and waves his arms.) Cut it out. Okay, I'll talk for a little longer. (He gets up and moves through the crowd to get away from B.) You know, it occurs to me, there is a story from my earlier childhood, before kindergarten, which I should tell.

B: Is this about stampeding giraffes in the womb? Good God what an asshole!

TB: (Throws his hand into the air in a gesture of defiance.) Stop it! (Pauses and regains his composure, slips into a half-smile. He circles the group as he begins his story.) My father took me and my brother out for a ride in grandfather's buggy (he bounces as though riding). We were bouncing along and all of a sudden we hit a big hole. The buggy lurched and I shot up and was about to fall over the side when my dad reflexively grabbed me. (Now he acts out that grab.) It seemed as natural as breathing to him. He just reached over and grabbed me. I could have fallen out and broken my neck; I could have been killed.

C: (Turns her attention to TB.) You really think about death a lot. You see every event, it seems, as a life or death event. My God, I can see why as childhood recedes you become more and more threatened. You can't go back; and even if you could, there's a gorilla at the end of the hall.

TB: More therapy! (Walks around the stage from person to person.) You know I took Psychology in college and went around analyzing everyone, too, (then takes on an air of seriousness—looks toward but beyond 30W). I am (but slows down and emphasizes his words or her words) "aware of death," but any sensible person is aware that everything is dying all the time.

M: (firmly—sits up straight). And being born.

TB: I don't know about that.

I: (beginning to get impatient) Are the stories over? Is it time to get to the point?

C: No, I think we've a ways to go.

TB: After I nap (heads back toward the couch).

B: (grabs him by the shoulder and spins him around)
I don't think so. (in TB's face) Talk now, sleep
later (shoves him).

TB: (pleadingly) I'm so tired.

I: (in an informative manner) If you don't deal
with us here, we'll invade your sleep. Here you
stand a chance, it's obvious you're somewhat in
control (looks around). But in your dreams we have
complete control. We tell the truth our way and you
cannot change anything. You are ours until you wake
up.

B: (cuts in) Yeah, we could have the gun bring you
home in a paper bag with a donut around your neck,
while ruptured appendixes dance in a conga line,
and ...

TB: (cuts him off) Threats to a tired man are
useless.

B: Threats are threats regardless. Go ahead! Go to
sleep!

I: Yes, go ahead.

TB: (Hesitates) Maybe a little longer. (He goes
to the refrigerator...) But I am allowed to have a
snack, (takes out a soda and drinks). I can go a
little longer as soon as the caffeine kicks in. (He
sips a bit more and belches, if possible.)

M: Toby!

F: That was uncalled for. You should be ashamed.

TB: (not paying attention to them) My sixth grade

year…

B: Thank you God! At least he didn't go month by
month or year by year.

CF: (across the stage from B, so spoken loudly,
almost defiantly) A story takes a long time.

M: (reflectively, as though she is remembering her
life) A long time to live, and a long time to tell.

C: (lifting his hand as though he is a schoolboy)
Is that because we have to make excuses or because
we have no first-hand witness present?

M: It's just that a story takes a long time.

TB: (moves in circles as he tells this, but
gravitates toward CF) In my sixth grade year, I
had the best teacher in the school. One day, when
I was coming back from the cafeteria, I was at the
head of my class with a couple of friends (looks
at CF). I popped a large, red, fire-hot jawbreaker into my mouth. I was in heaven until I accidentally swallowed it and it stuck in my throat.
I began to choke. I couldn't speak. I grabbed my
throat. I began to black out (uses hands as CF and
he act this out, swats his left hand to the side).
Johnny peeled off to go get the teacher. I swear,
I was starting to fall when Billy swatted me (CF
pops him) as hard as he could on my back. I coughed
(he coughs loudly) and that lawbreaker shot out
of my mouth like a bullet. My hands jerked out in
front of me and that jawbreaker smacked (smacks
one hand with the back of the other) into my hand.
I squeezed that killer ball while I took deep
breaths; I did not know how sweet air tasted until
that moment. I swore that I would never get rid of
that jawbreaker; I was going to keep it
forever. But as I stepped in the room, I tripped
and it shot out of my hand and rolled under the
bookcase (goes to coffee table and looks under it).

I started to reach under there to get it but the teacher came though the door then and told us to get in our seats for the weekly spelling test.

B: Gee, if you would have reached under there, you could have shown us your bronzed jawbreaker, sitting in your trophy case. (Holds his hands up, the left one palm up and the other as though holding the jawbreaker. He shows the invisible jawbreaker to everyone.)

CF: (Looks at B) That's uncalled for. (turning his attention back to TB) That was a scary experience.

TB: You know, I probably should have learned some great lesson from that experience, but all I learned is to be careful when you eat jawbreakers. In fact, I did not eat one for several years after that. Or ham!

30W: What? I don't follow that connection.

TB: (speaking to 30W) Oh, a couple of weeks later I swallowed some fat off a piece of ham I was chewing, but it was still connected to the ham. It dangled in my throat (making a gargling noise) and gagged me. I cleared my throat with all my might (which he does) until that fat vibrated back into my mouth (feigns a spit). Then I spit it out. I didn't eat ham for about four years.

I: I'm surprised you do anything.

C: Maybe he doesn't (stands quickly, to punctuate his sentiment).

TB: (emphatically) I'll have you remember that I have a job. (less forceful, but meant as a positive statement) I eat ham…now!

I: But, is there any risk in your life? (Stands up

and acts out cutting ham). Don't you cut your ham into teeny pieces after you have cut away any shred of fat? Isn't your job mundane and mindless, … absolutely meaningless? Don't you…

B: This is ridiculous. We're talking about how eating ham is some grand adventure.

30W: (hopeful with an implicit seduction) Are you through with your stories?

C and TB: (together while looking down) I don't think so. (C and TB look at each other)

TB: I do want to continue, because I know which story belongs next. A story of true friendship.

LL: (LL moves to the bathtub, closer to TB) Yes. Tell us one like that. These others have been so depressing.

TB: (a bit theatrical) My grade school years behind me, I moved to the scary world of junior high. I dreaded it. I was told that ninth graders roamed the halls looking for young kids to de-pants.

30W: (has to speak loudly over the music) De-pants?

TB: (Looking at 30W). Kids that would pull you in the bathroom, sometimes right in the hallway and take your pants off! Rumor had it they hung them up at the top of the flagpole for everyone to see. (B rolls his eyes—to B) Shut up.

LL: (looks shocked) They did what? (B mumbles and makes a motion with his hand so that it is clear he is indicating TB is nuts. TB senses this and speaks slowly at first)

TB: (speaks to LL for TB knows she is a

sympathetic audience) I found out they didn't do
it, at least as often as I thought. I thought
it was an everyday occurrence. You see, I was a
naïve and scared kid. Besides that, I was still so
self-conscious and ignorant about my body and the
changes which were taking place… and girls….. and
sex. I was very shy and easily shamed. That's where
George really helped (CF steps forward like a
champion and smiles).

B: (puts his hands to his head and shuts his eyes
as though he is receiving a vision) Is he.. Is he…
it's coming to me. Is he the guy who told you about
the (sarcastic) birds and the bees?

TB: No.

B: He showed you some filthy, pornographic pictures?

TB: No.

I: He got you laid.

TB: **No, no. He helped me understand myself, he
helped me understand my body.**

D: (becomes rigid, but also like he's ready to
attack) How? What are you talking about? Be more
specific (getting louder)? Did he teach you to play
with yourself? Did he play with you (starting toward CF but M restrains him)?

TB: (holds up a hand). Hold on. It's not that way.
It seems so funny now. (He turns and looks as
though he can see the scene to his right) We were
standing out behind the cafeteria. We were just
wasting time, having a silly conversation before
our next class. All of a sudden I confessed that I
thought I was weird or perverse or something like
that. **He asked me ***CF: Why?***** (TB is going to
alternate between CF who is playing out his imagi-
native scene with them and LL who is listening

attentively.)

B: So?

TB: (perturbed) He asked me why. Well, you can't
understand my answer unless you realize that I was
a bedwetter or at least I thought of myself as one.
(acts this out) I remember standing every night
right in front of the toilet squeezing every last
drop out of my bladder. I slept with my brother and
if I peed in the bed he would complain to mom and
dad.

B: He'd get really pissed off, huh? (Laughs) Can we
cut to the chase? This is so silly and... juvenile.
You were, uh, you are some screwed up wacko!

TB: (with measured angry voice shouting down B)
Well, I told him, my friend, that I was beginning
to have problems again with staying dry at night.
He asked me **CF: What do you mean?** I went on
to tell him that there wasn't as much pee as it
was gooey stuff. I thought maybe I was sick and my
pee was thickening up. I probably had some disease! He asked me **CF: Does this "problem" occur
with a dream?** I was too ashamed to tell him that
I usually did dreams on those nights. I was so em-
barrassed, but this was my best friend, so I told
him one of the dreams. I knew these dreams, which
were about women and me, were a result of my lust.
That's what my father would say (looks away from
D). My attraction to girls and women was so strong,
so obsessive that this lust flooded my dreams. **B:
I'll say! (holds up hands in defense)** (continues
with determination, hurrying to the end) My parents
had warned me. I was being punished by God by
losing my bladder control. And on top of that I was
diseased—my pee was turning to glue! (anxious sigh)

LL: And?

    C: And?

I: C'mon!

30W: Well?

TB: He laughed (**CF laughs**).

B: He should have! You have to admit…

TB: (Quickly) He laughed and I wondered if I had
misjudged him. Was this my friend or not. He saw
the look on my face and stopped. He said: **CF: I
wasn't laughing at you. What is happening to you
is called wet dreams; you dream of some good-looking woman and then you shoot off in your sleep or
as you are waking up. Sometimes they are detailed,
you and she are getting it on. My dad told me about
them. Ain't they great?** I swear to God, when I
got saved by the power of Jesus, I didn't feel as
relieved as that moment when I found out I was
okay.

B: Everybody knows about wet dreams!

TB: (forcefully, to B) I didn't! (back to LL) I
think the most difficult part was the dream. Here I
was lusting after some woman and that was wrong. I
mean, in my sleep! I was so caught up in lust that
it invaded my sleep. I would be talking with some
woman I knew. We might be in a secluded section
of a store, we might be in a living room, we might
be in a hallway. When I started to leave, the hall
just wasn't big enough for me to get by her. The
hallway seemed to press us together and when that
happened I would start humping her. It could be
the girl across the street who loved to press her
tits against me and say: (LL changes her expression
to a sultry one and oozes this line as she sub-
tlety moves her body) **LL: You liked that didn't
you?** And I did. (30W begins to walk toward TB) Or
it could be a total stranger who would be casually
saying: (She brushes his crouch and moves in front
of LL toward TB) **30W: Excuse me** and (they act
it out) rubbing me at the same time, but

then I would wake up and be soiling my pajamas in a sort of (clearly two syllable pronunciation to imitate the rhythm of shooting off) rhyth-mic, help-less, way. It felt good but was so evil. I was scared--wetting my pants and lusting at the same time. I was bound for hell.

B: I can't believe you were so stupid!

TB: (turns) I was shy and isolated (pushes 30W aside and takes a few steps toward LL) and scared and confused...

B: ...and horny! What you needed was a good feel (acts as though he is putting his hand up a skirt) in the afternoon behind junior high, not some friend to tell you what was going on in your sleep.

D: (like a preacher) No, he didn't need a cheap thrill, or (knowing that he didn't get the termi-nology right) whatever you called it. He was right to feel a little ashamed. Too bad he didn't know a little more about his body. And how God could help him.

LL: (curious) Do all guys have this happen?

CF: (takes charge) It's a stage moving from boyhood to manhood though even married men may have wet dreams. It's natural and nothing you should feel bad about. Maybe he was a little horny, but even that's natural. And (gets emphatic) it wasn't lust. Lust is conscious, lust is controlled, lust is a sort of rape. You jerk a woman off the street and stand her up in your imagination and use her for a prop.

30W: (flirtatiously) I wouldn't mind being a prop because I'm very proper?

B: Yeah! He sure propped himself up against her.

CF: You're crazy. He said he tried to get past her but that was impossible. They were thrown, or, at least, pressed together. What was he to do? Lust is making someone an object for selfish pleasure. When you lust, the woman, who is an object really, welcomes these advances, and goes wild just like you want her to. You control her. Wet dreams shouldn't be associated with lust; they possess an uncontrolled, uncontrollable character. It's as though fate has thrown you together. Wet dreams are gifts, and great fun (pause). You were lucky to have him for a friend.

B: I think you're crazy (to both CF and TB).

C: Is there anything to add to that story?

TB: (surprised) Not really. I just really wish that I could have had that friend some other time in my life. I wish he hadn't of moved away. Boy, the summer I worked on the hospital grounds crew, he could have helped me with my foreman. (B takes the stance of someone resting on his rake handle. He feigns smoking and just looking around into the audience, stopping for a moment when he sees a woman.) I hoed around the small trees while he watched the teenage girls walking down the street to a nearby swimming pool. When I finished I asked for a new assignment. He was staring intently so I followed his eyes and saw a shapely girl walking to the pool and she wore a tiny bikini; she almost looked naked. He looked at me, winked and said **B: What an ass!** I mentioned I knew her and his eyes narrowed. He said: **B: Go get her and bring her out back in the woods. I show you what a real man does.*** I was shocked. He laughed and said **B: You probably think your pecker is just to piss through.** He laughed again and told me to go water the trees along the emergency entrance. I turned to look at him as I left and he was (B rubs his crouch) rubbing his crotch and mumbling.

C: (looks around) What did you think about that girl? (TB winces)

M: (quickly and quietly) I think we ought to leave this subject behind.

D: I'll say.

LL: I just didn't know all that went on in a boy's head. My thoughts seem so tame compared to yours.

TB: (looking at her, defensively) Remember, it was not me that wanted to, uh...

B: ...do her, screw here, fuh...

D: (gesturing) Whatever! Leave it behind (hurriedly) Are you through?

TB: (Breathes a sigh of relief. Looks around as though he is trying to find his way or regain his direction or find that friend who, so long ago, was understanding. He moves into a more reflective pose. He has certainly been genuflecting but now he almost goes back in time as some images from the past are flushed up much like wild birds.) Miss Logan.

M: (like she didn't hear him) What? (more pointedly) Who? (hoping to lead him away from the "lust-filled" narrative)

TB: (matter of factly) Miss Logan. (M Tenses) Wow, I guess that crush started in fourth or fifth grade. So tall and full. Blonde and a broad smile which revealed the whitest teeth.

B: This guy thinks too much. And he works at a bakery all night? And then not even where you have to think, (speaks in a sing-song voice) mixing dough, cutting doughnut holes, dropping them in the hot oil, get them out, coat them with the glaze, and do it again and again and again. Didn't you go to college? Must have gotten a (linger between B.A. and D) B.A.D.—Bachelor of Arts in Donuts. (laughs)

TB: (continues as though he did not hear B, his back was to him). 30W mimes the part of Miss Logan) I would sit in vocal music with Miss Logan at the piano and imagine our long life together. I would have to grow up first, of course.I could just imagine her kissing me and that was bliss. And when she stood up to her full height, about 5'10", I was looking right at her breasts. I would follow the lines of her body up and down, finally shifting my eyes in a sort of ritual between her face, especially her moving lips, her breasts and her hips. I watched her every move; I did everything she commanded (short pause). She eventually got married and I found a hundred things wrong with her. Besides, I had fallen for the woman next door… and her good-looking daughter, Leanne. (pauses then emphatically)I longed for Leanne. She was a "nice" girl; she was beyond reproach.

D: (sensing ridicule) What's wrong with that phrase?

M: If everyone were beyond reproach we would have a marvelous world.

I: People beyond reproach are not a part of this world.

D: People beyond reproach clean up the world after others have trashed it (glares at I).

TB: (stands still as though seeing this in his mind, but he looks at LL from time to time)I'm just saying that she was like a goddess…you know, distant but desirable. I would watch her mow the grass in her tight blue gym shorts; I would watch her lay in the sun in her yard. (LL begins to act out the girl while Toby plays his part) One time, about 9:30 at night, I was walking home from a friend's house. As I got close to Leanne's house, I was cutting across her lawn, I sensed there was more light then usual. I looked up and (looks at LL) and golly (LL acts this out) there stood Leanne in her lighted room in her panties and just a bra. I guess she had been in a hurry or some- thing and forgot to shut the curtains. I stared for a moment before I realized what I was doing. I was afraid she would see me and tell her mother, so I ran.

M: Well, for whatever reasons you made a good decision.

D: (cuts in) However, as soon as you looked, you shouldn't have stared at all. (almost like a preacher) Always flee temptation! Always!

TB: I think she did look out the window; I don't know if she saw me. I ran into my yard, low to the ground, as though I was in combat and I didn't want to be seen. (moves to the couch bent low and turns) When I got to my room, I must have sat there for an hour trying to relive that moment, trying to flash back in my mind to that figure, that body, that uncovered body. I thought about going back out- side and sneaking, maybe crawling, across her yard to see her slip her bra off (LL acts as though she does). (LL acts out his description) I knew she had probably pulled the curtains together or turned off the light. When I went to bed, I could not quit thinking about her.

30W: Lord, what an imagination. I don't require imagination, well, it does liven up the encounters.

B: Lord, what a frustrated, horny kid!

TB: (As though he is in competition with himself) That's nothing. Once when they were gone for an afternoon and I was the only one at my house, I saw that those shorts had dropped off the clothesline in the backyard. (creeps out between coffee table and bathtub) I crept over there and grabbed them and brought them to my bedroom. (runs and hides behind couch) I took off all my clothes and put them on. I got so hard! All of a sudden I thought I saw a spot on them. I got scared, so I jerked them off and threw back on my clothes. (runs back) I ran outside and hung them up. I didn't see a spot then. For weeks I was paranoid, I thought she knew what I had done. And maybe she had told her mother. (pause—LL takes on a more mature look in her face) Her mother was just like her, beautiful and friendly, you know, (emphasis) beyond reproach. She was very religious. But one time I saw her working in her flower garden in short shorts and a halter top. I wondered how a nice woman could dress like that? That confused me. (LL gets to her hands and knees as though she is working in the garden) I can still see her leaning over, her thighs growing taunt, her breasts hanging down as her halter top gaped. They seemed to be growing right before my eyes. I was walking through her yard. When I was about ten feet from her, she heard me and looked up (LL lifts her head). She smiled (LL smiles) and said hello. I said hello, but my eyes were locked on her breasts. In my mind I ran over, unclasped the top, watched it fall to the ground, and her breasts swing clear. I dropped to my knees and began to fondle and kiss her breasts (looks around at everyone looking at him, even LL as he moves back to reality). Then, I noticed she was looking at me very intently (LL continues to act out this narrative.) She stood up and started to wipe her forehead, but I saw she wasn't sweating. I thought she did that because she knew I was looking. I told her I had to meet a friend and ran off (TB moves back); my face was burning with embarrassment. (he eventually circles around behind the couch) I went down the street and circled back to hide behind a bush to see if she would lean over again.

I: You know if you carried a bush with you, you

wouldn't have to run anywhere to hide!

TB: (waves off I and continues) She was gone when I looked. I waited five or ten minutes. When she came out of the house; she was wearing a white sleeveless blouse.(with an immense sense of embarrassment) She knew! (pause) I shut my eyes and tried to remember what I had seen. (He looks up) I thought about her and her daughter all the time.

M: (disgusted—behind TB) This is nasty. Do you have to talk about this and go on and on?

30W: (somewhat puzzled) All of this is natural and you act like it is unnatural (M gives her a judgmental look).

B: It is pathetic isn't it?

D: It's pathetic and sinful (seemingly agreeing with B)!

B: I mean he never gets to grab tit!

TB: That's all I need,(looks at D and M) puritans and (looks at B) degenerates (firmly). I will go on. (with determination) I always thought Leanne would come home from college and see this kid next door, me, who was now a man, and strike up a conversation. She would realize that I was an intelligent, witty guy whom she had overlooked. I knew she would fall in love with me. That may have been my wildest fantasy, because I believed it could actually happen. (pause, a hurt chuckle, then slowly) It never happened, of course.

B: You have been a frustrated, horny kid your whole life, haven't you?

TB: Every desire or fantasy of mine is just a sign of horniness to you, isn't it?

B: I don't know about that, but I do know that a little pussy would have pleased your johnson!

TB: (judgmentally). You are so crude!

B: Hey! I can't help it if you try to make all this "desire," you call it, into some kind of deeply meaningful stuff. The formula, as I see it, is this— If you like what you see (some sort of suggestive hand missions, and the juices are flowing (maybe a body motion that can transform, with the next half-line, to a suggestive back-and-forth movement), then you need some action. But, you keep it all in your head (motion of cramming it on one's head and this motion will shift to horns with the next line). You're going to grow horns, buddy (then he acts as if TB's head explodes).

TB: (defensively) I admit I've always been fasci-nated by the opposite sex...

B: (echoes him sarcastically) "fascinated by the opposite sex!" That sounds like you work with laboratory specimens.

TB: (loudly but almost like he is talking to him-self) Even in first grade I told a girl if she would kiss me on the lips I would give her a ten cent roll of candy...

B: Prostitution!! You were dealing with hookers before you could hook up!

TB: ...but it wasn't what I expected, so I demanded my candy back.

B: Did you get it?

TB: No, I chased her all recess period but I never could catch her.

B: If you didn't sit around dreaming about all this

sex, you would be in better shape. Then you could
have caught her.

TB: Give me a break! I was curious. I saw people
kiss all the time on television and it looked like
fun. But I didn't find it all that pleasurable in
the first grade.

B: "All that pleasurable."

TB: Quote making fun of me!

C: (cutting in) Toby. You're drifting. Are you
through with your stories? Are you ready to talk
straight?

TB: You **want** me to be out of stories, but I'm not
through. It's the interruptions that cause me to
drift. I had finally started to develop momentum
when this specialist on horniness started bugging
me. All of you had let me go, for the most part,
except him. If he shuts up, I'll finish much quicker. (B rolls his eyes and starts to speak but C
gestures him to move back.)

B: (over his shoulder) Okay, the gorilla is caged.

TB: What if he gets out.

B: Well, you've got your gun. (This stops TB.)

TB: (Slower, more pronounced in his pace) Of course
all my contacts with Leanne or her mother and
others were in my imagination. And it wasn't overly
erotic; I didn't masturbate yet.

B: (Muffled) Who would have guessed it?

TB: (defensive) I was old enough but I was taught
that it just wasn't nice to touch THAT (looks down)
for THAT purpose and think those thoughts for THAT
purpose. I know it sounds crazy, but that's the way

I thought for that was what I was taught at home
and at my church. Sexual stuff was for married
people. Eventually I did begin to date. That was
difficult for me. I was shy and my parents wouldn't
allow let me go to the dances at school. My
mother used to say **M: A dancing foot and a pray-
ing knee don't go on the same leg**. I couldn't
go to drive-ins; I couldn't go to pool halls. I
couldn't go where most of my friends could go, I
COULD go to anything at the church. Mom wanted
me to date a nice church girl. That added to my
problems. You didn't date church girls, you just
showed up, sat by the one you liked, and grinned
a lot. Then you went home. That's what I did but
I got tired of that. Who makes up these rules?
(laughs suddenly) Just the other night this guy
walks up to me ("I" walks over to TB) at work and
says: **I: You're the intellectual around here;
let me ask you a question. Which is the most harm-
ful—to stand here and smoke a cigar and blow the
smoke in your face or to stand here naked and talk
to you?**. Well, I hate smoke. So, I told him, the
smoker. He replied: **I: Then why do we have so
many laws against nudity and so few against people
belching smoke into our faces?** ("I" moves to the
side) There it is. Who makes the rules?

C: I have a question, too.

TB: (warily) What is it?

C: Which is more dangerous, to buy a loaf of bread
or to buy a gun?

TB: (visibly angry) A LOAF OF BREAD IF YOU'RE NOT
GOING TO GET ROBBED! (pause). And I got robbed my
senior year. I had a four-point average. The valedictorian got to address the whole senior class at
graduation and tell everyone what the world was
really about. I wanted to speak so I **had** to have
the perfect average. All through school, the
pressure had been unbelievable. Even a B+ meant I

wouldn't be the valedictorian and I wouldn't have a place on the podium. (with disgust and disappoint-ment in his voice) Then, the principal decided to let the senior class vote to select the speaker that year. He said the seniors deserved to pick the person from their class whose opinion they respect-ed the most. He probably did that because there were three valedictorians. (emphatically) None of us got picked. I sat there with everyone else. (sighs) Who makes the rules? Why, when you work so hard, when you prepare so much in advance, when you give up everything for a goal, is it snatched from you? (TB now becomes silent and goes back to the couch after acting out most of this story. He flops down and places his heads in his hands as his elbows rest on his knees. Almost inaudibly, he speaks) I'm through.

I: (Taken by surprise like everyone who had listened but had listened rather disinterested-ly—scattered about, standing and sitting. Everyone felt this storytelling would go on much longer.) What? Just like that? No big finish?

TB: I'm through. You know, with a whimper. That's it.

I: Wait, wait, wait. Didn't you go to college? There ought to be a couple of good stories from there. If you went to college, you got away from your parents and all those church girls. Didn't you date there? (saucily) Maybe catch up, you know?

D: (lecturing to I, almost like a commercial) Yes, college. The college degree can be the secret of a successful life, to earning a good living, to getting the job you want.

TB: Sure. More school, more degrees, more promises, more disappointments. So why continue talking about it?

C: That didn't stop you from telling these other stories.

TB: I said that I'm through.

C: (almost to himself) So, those other stories weren't revelations at all; (walks a few steps to the side) they were attempts to get away. (louder) Why talk about college when you have to talk about what happened after college, when you have to talk about now. (moving a couple of steps toward TB) Is that it?

TB: (pensively, to himself before he can stop himself) Right. I mean, my college experience was the same as everyone else's.

B: No, it wasn't. I don't know anyone that is as messed up as you. Your earlier life was not like everyone else's and you surely didn't spare us any of the details.

TB: (Abruptly, but slightly sing-song). Okay, okay, so I went to college (he gets up). Yeah I got dates. The first girl I dated swore I was God's gift to her. She broke up with this guy she had dated for three years and chased me around campus. She was too forward. **B: Missed a chance there, dude!** The second girl I dated (30W moves to the couch and sits down) seemed to really like me. (he moves to beside her on the couch and puts his arm around her) One night in the car in front of this girl's dorm, we kissed a lot, (slowly like he was bragging) a lot and did some things my parents said were for married people.

B: Like what?

TB: Like French kissing.

B: Good grief. What an amateur!

TB: (While he speaks 30W scoots real close and looks at him with interest) I didn't really know much more then I did in junior high. You know in seventh grade I told Stan Oliver that when two people got married, God set special processes in motion and the woman got pregnant at God's pleasure. People couldn't guess how many kids they would have because God planned that stuff. Stan looked at me a long time then said I was crazy. So, I asked him how babies got started. He stared at me through his thick glasses that had slipped down his nose and sputtered through his buck teeth: **B: You're wrong; your dad fucked your mother.** I was shocked. I said: "He did not. My father would never do that to my mother." He replied: **B: Oh yes he did and if you don't believe me go ask him. ** I couldn't ask my Dad (awkwardly silly) did you fuck mom, he would a killed me. Somehow I knew he was mostly telling the truth.(Pause)(TB becomes focused on 30W) So, here I am in college and this woman is sticking her tongue in my mouth. That would have thrilled old Stan Oliver. I was both thrilled and scared. I stopped and moved backwards. I looked at her and told her I really liked her.(30W acts this out) She glared at me dumbfounded; she sort of let out a nervous laugh. She shrugged her shoulders and said: **30W: Hey this is for fun. You're not getting involved are you? I don't want to get involved. C'mon back over here.*** I felt so foolish, so naïve, so suddenly dead. My innocence melted away like some candy coating. I managed a laugh and some smart reply, but my mind exploded with pain and confusion and rejection. I was completely overwhelmed; I didn't know what to say. She just stared at me and asked if I was okay. I said yeah even though I was lost, but I shoved down the feelings,took a deep breath and scooted back over. We frenched and groped for another forty-five minutes. I kissed her over and over again, mechanically thrusting my tongue in her mouth while my hands searched her body (rubs her breasts and waist and the thigh closest to him crossing to the

other thigh and hip) for I don't know what. I
started getting really mad, too. Finally, (aside)
I'd heard about this from my buddies when they came
in from their dates, (he pulls his hand back to the
near thigh, down to her exposed knee and then
under her skirt) I slip my hand under her skirt, up
the top of her thigh. She sighed and slid down in
the seat (30W complies). I felt her underwear. She
thrust her belly out so I would put my hand down
her panties and I began to...I didn't know what the
hell I was going to do; I didn't know what to do.
And when I touched her pubic hair, it startled me.
My hand shot back (he pulls his hand out as though
it has a mind of its own) as though I had touched
a hot stove. I couldn't stop myself. It was like a
reflex. I can still hear the elastic of her panties
snapping back. She gave me the oddest look. I was
so nervous I began to shout: (shouts) "I've got to
go back and study. (looks at his wrist) I didn't
know it was so late." Then I jumped out of the car,
ran around (runs around couch), and jerked open her
door. (TB shoves her to the side of the stage) I
walked her back to the dorm as quickly as I could,
I mean I was pulling her along, while I mumbled
about all the work I had to do. I left her at the
door and ran back to my car.

LL: Maybe she had been hurt and didn't want to be
hurt again. Maybe that's why she was so cool and
mechanical. And you reacted to her in the same way.

I: Maybe she just wanted to have some fun, like she
said.

M: I don't think she was a very nice girl. You know
you can't get to love by physical means. **Commitment**
comes first, **then** love, (quitter and a bit embar-
rassed) then the physical, er, activities.

TB: (looking at his mother like he was a little
boy) She was one of the sharpest girls on campus.
I thought our kissing did mean something. It did

for me until she hurt me.

30W: She didn't mean to hurt you. It happens all the time. You were just naïve, obviously, and she didn't hurt you, didn't cause you get hurt, you did that, you caused your pain.

LL: Yes, getting hurt just happens and you have a share in it. And you have to learn that; you need to understand that.

TB: Just be quiet. I told you I didn't want to talk about college. College was a continuation of what had already happened to me. Promises, dreams, disappointments. I don't need to give you the details. You get a degree that is suppose to be your ticket to success and happiness, but it has never got me any breaks. You look for someone to marry, and all you find are people torn up inside and they can't care for anyone else. It's a mess I could have done without!

C: (like a statement) So you've had it?

TB: (So worked up that he can't stop) Yes, I've had it. I want to go on record. The stories are over. This is the epilogue.

C: Epilogues many times lead to the heart of the story.

TB: (moves toward C throughout this speech) Oh, shut up. What do you know? Who are you to suggest that this will get to the "heart of the story?" I am fed up with your...your...your presumed omniscience, your presumptuousness, your presence. I wanted to be left alone, but since you (gestures to everyone) were here I entertained you. I told my story.

B: You entertained us? That's your story? What a waste of time!

D: (defensively) That's not all the story because your story is only a part of the whole...

C: (looks around) Stop it, everyone. Stop this bickering. It's pointless.(looks at TB, moving closer to him) And so are your stories, Toby. We want to know what started all this.(looks at the gun) We are not going away until you tell us. We don't care about your stories, we want to know **why** you told these stories. We want some directness. If you want to try to make us believe that these stories were randomly thrown out as some sort of entertainment, go ahead. But we are not naïve. You can tell us more stories, you can choose to do that. You can also choose to stop the stories and talk to us directly, truthfully.

TB: I don't think you understand how much pressure I live with.

C: So what's your point?

B: You're stalling.

M: Relax and tell us what is really on your mind.

I: Come on.

TB: Okay, just let me have a little... (he waves his hand knowing that to call for quiet one more time will be unbearable) more time. I guess the biggest disappointment was my academic work in college. (B throws up his hands) I went from a 4.0 in high school to a 2.9 my first semester in college. (Throughout this next conversation TB moves from one character to another trying to answer their questions or objections.)

M: A 2.9? That's not bad.

D: A lot of people would be proud to have...

TB: (to D and M) Shut up! A 2.9 was lousy to me. I was doing lousy.

M: You felt like you weren't doing well.

TB: I was doing lousy. I expected to do as well as before, as in high school. College owed me that. But I was doing lousy.

30W: Is that the average you had when you graduated?

TB: (to 30W) No, I had a 3.1845

B: Gee, you should have worked it out to seven places.

LL: (waves B off, she is trying to help) Doesn't that mean you graduated with honor?

TB: (to LL) I graduated Cum Laude at my college. So what! Many of my friends graduated Magna and Summa Cum Laude.

LL: All of them?

TB: No. But the people I identified with the most did. My suitemate, three or four guys I studied with.

LL: What else was so bad?

TB: My major was a bust. I started in biology but I made a B so I switched to psychology. Those guys were nuts and, besides, I started diagnosing everybody, and everybody was either crazy or dangerous. (pause, then with a bit of whimsy) I was crazy. I kept searching for the major that I could do really well in. I came to the end of my sophomore year without a major. You have to have a major by the end of sophomore year. The next on my list was history, the record of failures for mankind? But

I said, why not? History became my major. Now I
couldn't turn back. If I made a B, or less, and I
did, I had to grit my teeth and bear it. There was
no turning back, none. And then, bang (as he claps
his hands), "Toby Barrister, (whispered as though a
curse) Cum Laude." And then I was nowhere. Nowhere.
No job. Nobody to marry. I mean what can you do
with a history major other than teach, do research
and write another history book?

D: It seems to me that a history degree would be a
perfect background for any number of jobs. I mean,
what about law? How many of your friends became
lawyers?

TB: (to D) Law! Three more years of cramming. I
wanted to be through; I wanted to be prepared. I
didn't want a "perfect background."

D: You have to be flexible. You have to adapt yourself to what's out there.

TB (to 30W) YOU can adapt. I wanted a life. I wanted a job. I had an education and I wanted a job
which fit me.

C: Is that why you've gone from job to job for over
7 years. Is that why you're a baker's assistant at
the Jolly Donut bakery and have been for the last
three years?

TB: (compliant) That's why. I've been in fast foods
and slow foods, in the motels and hotels and
whoretels, in furniture moving, in weight control,
in travel and on welfare. I even started an
encounter group. Mostly I've been in hiding. I
don't keep in touch with anyone, except my parents.
And I always visit them in their home. I save or
borrow enough money to go in the style I've accus-
tomed them to expect. I've been at this address a
year after being evicted from a better place in a
better location and I've never let them visit me

here,...or anyplace. They don't know what I really do.

B: (sarcastic) What do you do? Have your mail sent to a real expensive home and hurry over there to pick it up before the butler comes.

TB: No. I have a post office box, but my address is Toby Barrister, Barrister, Inc, P.O. Box 75, and you know the rest.

M: Don't you think you ought..er, I mean, when will you tell them that you, you have, have this job, this, you had…

D: (moving slightly toward TB as he does when he gets angry, e.g. with B before) This is disgrace-ful! It's lying. It's just plain lying! How can you face yourself? This is not what you were taught!

M: You really ought not be ashamed; maybe you're just having trouble getting started.

B: Getting started? For seven years he's just had trouble getting started? (rubbing it in) Ever since you've graduated from college you've been a bum. Have you really tried?

I: He's got a point. We shouldn't lie to him and hide the truth like he has chosen to do. He's inept or scared or lazy or something. Why waste time and words; he's a loser.(directs hf to TB) You're a loser.

CF: Wait a minute!

LL: Don't be so harsh!

D: Hold on!

M: You didn't mean that!

TB: I am not a loser!

C: (yelling, trying to get control—moving to the center as he speaks) No, no, no. All this is too simple, too simple. Toby is coming to grips with his sad life. These stories are key. Look at them; he has never been at home in the world. But I think today is going to be an important day. I think he is going to get straightened out today. I think he knows that. I think that is why he told us these stories, parts of his story. He wanted to let us in on why he is so troubled. And I think Toby is ready to make his peace, to tell us things he's never told anyone, even his parents, aren't you? Are you ready?

TB: I think so.

C: (moves closer to TB) The answer is yes. Are you ready? (growing louder)

TB: I think so. (growing louder)

C: (stops walking—forceful) The answer is yes. Are you...

TB: (Yelling) Yes! (then trailing off) Yes, yes, yes, yes, yes, yes.

C: So why did you buy the gun?

TB: (Slowly, but not apologetically) I thought I might like to kill myself. (The group which has been marginally interested or interested from time to time turns when he says this. They are caught off-guard, surprised, shocked. They make sounds which reveal their surprise. As the following people speak TB moves to the couch.)

M: What?

B: What kind of line is that? Is this more of the

bullshit that you've been throwing out all morning? (mocking) "I thought I might like to kill myself." Nobody likes to kill themselves; they may do it but they don't like doing it.

I: They might.

B: Shut up. And what's more, if you're going to kill yourself, why waste all our time with these stories which make absolutely no sense.(looking at C)I don't doubt that you're mixed up, that's obvious. But killing yourself? Good God!

C: (to B) Open your eyes. Don't you see what those stories were? They were to allow Toby to face the truth. They weren't really for our information. He told those stories so that he could see he had **had** it; he bought a gun to finish his story, to (emphasizes the "p"), punctuate the final chapter.

LL: How do you know?

C: (moves toward LL)Have you ever heard that as someone is dying, maybe in an accident or even from a disease, that their life passes before them.

LL: Yeah, but I don't think that applies here.

C: You're wrong. Look at it.(Looks at TB affectionately; TB sits on the couch rather like a zombie). Toby has made his life, or parts of it, pass before him. Now he is ready to die.

M: (moves up behind TB) But people who see their lives pass before them want to live. They tell others later about that vision, about their life passing before them. That is how they cling to life in the face of death.

C: Toby has clung to death in the middle of life and he's tired of hanging on.

D: (Everyone seems to talk over TB) This can't be true, can it Toby? (pause) Speak up, boy!

CF: There's got to be another interpretation.

C: (Sternly, but gently, as a father) Toby.

TB: (quickly) He's right. (Then more slowly) I bought the gun to kill myself. Today. I've had it.

M: You're tired. You said so yourself. Go to bed. Everything will be better in the morning.

B: Yeah. Among the doughnuts life takes on new meaning.

M: Hush!

B: You hush! If this sucker wants to kill himself, let him. I can't stand anymore of his pitiful stories, his disgusting complaints.

D: Wait a minute. Let's slow down and let Toby talk. Let's hear what he has to say.

C: Yes, let's, (accusingly), but let's not put words in his mouth. Let's not cover over his pain. Let's not overlook **his decision.**

D: Who are you to tell me what to do.

I: (all the speakers are slowly moving toward the center as though an actual collision will take place) He's the one who made Toby tell the truth, that's who he is. And, I might add, he did it.

D: He's the one who has **put** a notion into the boy's (halts, realizing he has turned Toby into an abstracted person), uh, Toby's head.

B: Did he put the gun in the bag?!? Did he buy the gun?!?

M: Toby bought that for protection! He said that!

B: He also said he wanted to kill himself and admitted that was the true reason he bought the gun.

C: Hold it, hold it. Let's let Toby talk. He's the key. Toby?

TB: (They turn and look at TB; he speaks slowly) I bought the gun so that I could kill myself and that's that.

LL: No!

    D: No, that's wrong.

        M: You're tired; get some sleep.

D: For heaven's sake, no one in their right mind commits suicide. Talk to someone.

    LL: Don't even think of doing...that.

        CF: That would be a tragic
        mistake, a waste.

D: Where you would get an idea like that, I don't know. You kids get so depressed when the times get the least bit tough. In World War II things got desperate...

TB: (he stands up and moves toward the side) Please, not another "WWII" story.

D: Well, we didn't give up. That's the point. We never gave up.

M: You really can't mean you want to kill yourself.

TB: (still focusing on D's remarks, he turns and faces D): Maybe you did give up but you don't remember it. Maybe you gave up but the war came to an end before you died. Just because you survived, you think you're some kind of hero.

D: That's not true!

LL: (all these speakers moving toward TB) You really can't mean you want to kill yourself.

> M: You are such a darling; you mean the world to everyone.

> D: (a little stern) When did you start being so confused. Where on earth did you get this idea of suicide?

> M: (quickly coming back to her theme) You can talk to anyone who knew you when you were growing up and they thought you were so nice and well-behaved. And so promising (realizing she was speaking in the past tense) Or, ask your friends now. They would say the same, I'm sure.

> LL: (passionately) All of us have times when we feel low. You must keep going.

> I: (brashly — he stops all of their movements toward TB. All eyes focus on her) I can see where he could get such an idea! This is a lousy world full of lousy people. Who really cares? All any of you care about is keeping this guy living so you won't have to face the absurdity of his life and the absurdity of your attempt to keep him clinging to it. I say if the guy wants to kill himself, let him. If he thinks he is a loser, he is a loser. If he wants to get out, let him get out. Think about him. He's an adult; let him go. (ends rather powerfully, triumphantly)

(Everyone seems to be taken aback—some because she

speaks for suicide, others because she speaks so
suddenly and strongly.)

D: (charges I) Wait just a minute! How can you be
so irresponsible! We're dealing with a tired,
confused person (points his head toward TB) and you
try to make this decision seem like, like...(waves
his hand as he thinks) choosing a channel on the
television.

I: Shove it!

D: You see how disrespectful…

I: (cuts in with the first two or three words coming
in a slow measured pace) You listen to him, then
listen to me. I'm serious about Toby, so serious
that I take him literally. I don't put on him my
idea of what life should be. I offer him the freedom, and the support to do what he must.

M: (coming up just behind and to the side of D) You
have some nerve to suggest that suicide is just
another decision. It's a terribly final one.

CF: Hey, hey! All of us need to slow down.

TB: That's right. I wish all of you would just be
a little quieter so that I can think. I need to
think.

M: Sleep is more important right now.

> I: You don't need to think. Thinking
> wastes time.

> B: Right!

I: You know what is right for you. Do it (starts a
litany which will try to drown out the persons she
disagrees with and provide background for the ones
"on her side."), do it, do it, (B joins) do it, do

it...

M: No! Go to bed.

    D: At least rest some.

CF: ...and don't pay any attention to those who would push you into doing something rash.

    I: Staying alive is something rash for him.

        LL: Quit being so ugly.

      D: (both a command and a suggestion) Rest.
        M: Lay on the couch.

      B: Get on with it.

TB: (Suddenly, after turning away during their continued bickering, he whirls around.) Shut up! (They all draw back as if scolded and freeze until his last word in the speech. Toby goes back to the coffee table, basically in the middle, and walks back and forth as though he is a caged beast. He runs his fingers through his hair so that it becomes quite messed up.) (after a while) I swear to God; all of you act as though you cared for me but you are all caught up in some debate that seems to ignore me. Hey. I'm right here. I'm Toby and I'm considering suicide. You turn it into some kind of intellectual argument you want to win, some abstract issue you want to resolve in your own way. It isn't an intellectual problem; it isn't some abstract issue. I have a problem with my life; I don't like it. I don't like living. I don't want to go on.

I: There. You see. Don't jump down my throat. I'm the one listening.

C: He's right, you know. Toby has made a decision

and we must respect it whatever the consequences.

M: But anyone saying what Toby is saying cannot be in his right mind!

C: Why not?

M: Because people in their right minds want to live!

C: Because you say so! (takes on the guise of a TV preacher) You remind me of one of those guys in an evangelistic group who goes to the beach to tell people about Jesus. They walk up to people and ask them if they are happy. If the people say they are, these (sarcastically) "saviours" tell them that they are not really happy, they just think they are happy. Well, I say, what's the difference in being happy and thinking that you're happy? (Hurries on before any can reply and waves his arm to keep them from interrupting. Puts his arm around the shoulders of TB and parades him around from person to person to make his point.) **This** man bought a gun. **This** man brought this gun home. **This** man is tired, not from lack of sleep, but because his life is meaningless—he says its worthless. **This** man says it **ain't worth living**. He feels that from the inside out, (looks at Toby) and he felt it so strongly that before he expressed what he was going to do, he prepared to do something. He bought a gun, he brought the gun home, now he's going to use it on himself. WE SHOULDN'T STAND IN HIS WAY!

D: For God's sake, man, don't you see what you are saying. You are an agent of death! Stop it!

M: For Toby's sake, stop it.

LL: Yes! When someone is dying, trapped somewhere, perhaps in the rubble of an earthquake, you tunnel to them, you do whatever you have to do to save them. Toby is covered up. (moving toward TB

but not nearly the whole way) We must open a way to
him. We can't turn our backs now and later erect
a monument to a man who (gestures as she imitates
reading an inscription) "got covered up and maybe
he wanted it that way."

C: But those people you're talking about (mutters)
again (picks back up the pace) are ones who want to
live. Toby does not want to live. It's not "maybe
he wanted it that way;" **he does**. Perhaps, just perhaps, there are people in earthquakes who choose
that time to give up. They could be saved but they
see it as a good time to die. If we save them, they
hate us. Maybe there are people alive today just
like that. We should have let them die. We need to
let Toby die.

D: What utter nonsense...utter nonsense.

LL: I can't understand how anyone could say such
things.

M: (imploringly) Toby, get some rest.

CF: Shut us all out.

TB: How can I?

C: Why should you? Come on, Toby. Stay the course.
Don't miss the chance. You have told us your
story, don't forget that. And don't forget what
you've just told us. Remember and act. Do it (looking at I).

B: (in an affected tone like a radio announcer) And
now the last episode in that tale of woe—The
suicide of Toby.

C: (before the sarcasm of B's remark can soak in, C
salvages his train of thought. They all start
arguing around TB) Toby. Feel the sadness of your
own stories; remember that sadness and do what you

must).

D: (as though he suddenly received an insight which will change the whole scene) Wait a minute. He did not tell the whole story. What of all the moments he enjoyed.

C: Did he mention those? Did you hear any story not colored by disappointment or embarrassment or sadness or confusion?

D: No, not today, but on another day he would tell all those.

C: Would he? (more emphasis) Would he?

D: Of course he would.

      CF: I think he would.

            M: Most certainly.

      LL: He might tell them now.

            B: (Frustrated and Tired) Oh no.

      CF: Hush! Maybe he will tell them now.

        D: Tell us some more stories, stories when you were happy.

M: (emphatically) I think he is usually happy. Right now, he's just tired and frustrated and lonely...

C: No!. He's unhappy. Right now he may be tired and frustrated and lonely, but he is permanently unhappy. And he will continue to be tired and frustrated and lonely and (slows on the word) **unhappy** because he hates living.

D: He may be disappointed in the way his life has gone lately, but he can turn the corner. I don't think he hates living.

C: Turn the corner! Listen to him! (points to Toby)

M: Let him be. Let him rest.

C: I will let him rest, but the "rest" he chooses for himself. He wants a **permanent** rest, a rest that will end life.

LL: Death is not rest.

(Toby is up again and pacing and running his hands through his hair and shaking his head and getting more and more disturbed.)

C: How do you know?

M: She knows like I know. I just know. And I know that you have somehow manipulated Toby (short pause) toward a terrible choice. You're like those who encourage a person on a ledge to jump. The person on the ledge is still clinging to life; that person on the ground is merciless and cruel.

C: Toby was already moving toward the edge, has been for a long time. I just encouraged him to admit it. When he finally told us why he bought that gun, that was an act of courage. When he does it, when he pulls the trigger, that will be an act of courage. But all of you who would stop him are the ones who are troubling Toby. You are the manipulators.

D: Wait a minute. I don't think anyone who allows someone, Toby, to consider suicide without trying to stop him has his best interest in mind.

CF: Absolutely true.

LL: I tend to agree. You have to reach out.

M: You have to do what you can.

D: You can't allow them to do such a senseless and destructive act.

M: You have to help them choose to live.

LL: Nothing is hopeless!

I: (like cold water—abrupt and shocking) Some things are hopeless, believe me.

B: Like this guy.

M: You're wrong. And heartless. (maternally) You must watch what you are saying. (whispered) He is so troubled and until he can think straight we must watch what we say. Please!!

B: Don't whisper at me. The guy is a loser and you are part of the reason, you sentimental fake.

D: Nobody speaks like that to her. You better apologize...

M: What do you expect from him? Ignore him. It's dangerous to irritate him.

D: You're right. He's a merchant of death, a worthless bully.

C: (abruptly) Toby. Are you ready?

M: Wait a minute. I haven't finished. I want to know which of you doesn't agree with, I mean, doesn't think anyone, including Toby, should hill himself. Come over on this side. (The people begin to move)

C: Hold it. Hold it. This won't prove anything.

M: It will prove that you don't represent every-body.

B: Where does Toby stand?

I: Yeah.

C: (They look at him). That's what I'm been saying. Toby has the last word.

M: But we must encourage him to make the best decision.

C: That's what I'm trying to do. But what you mean is manipulate him.

M: No, I don't mean manipulate him. I mean help him.

B: (Parodies the "I can't pay the rent skit—first sarcastically) Help him! Help him!(forcefuly) Let him be. Help him! Help him! Let him be.(pause then pleadingly) Why not let the guy do what he wants to do. It's his life and his death.

D: Nobody's life is their own. We all affect one another.

B: I'm sick. (mocking) "Nobody's life is their own. We all affect one another." My life is mine and I will do what I damn well please with my life. And if anyone gets in my way they had better watch out. (raises his fist) I'll affect them.

D: You're blind.

B: No, you're blind and deaf.

D: (starts to charge) Why you...

M: (restrains D) I said ignore him.

C: Go ahead and ignore him. But quit ignoring the fact that Toby wants out.(his voice begins to rise). Toby, not me, wants out. Toby wants us out of the way. Toby wants all of us out of his way.

M: I just can't believe that he really wants to kill himself.

       LL: I have to agree.

          D: Well, anybody with any sense would agree.

I: I got lots of sense; I'm probably more intelligent than any of you and I say suicide is an option for anyone, or, everyone.

D: Not for me.

C: (cutting in) I don't think intelligence has much to do with it. But if you're listening at all, you know what Toby wants.

LL: You can hear people's words but feel deep inside what they are really saying or want to say. Toby is crying for help.

    M: Of course. That's what I've been trying to say.

C: You are putting words in his mouth, still projecting your agenda on Toby. Toby has been asking for privacy so that he could do what he must do.

M: Toby feels abandoned and if we abandon him now he will act out of despair. I can't let him do that. I won't leave him alone.

B: (quickly) You won't quit badgering him.

C: (quickly) You won't listen to him.

M: (slowly and firmly) I won't let him go.

I: All of this bickering is senseless. Let's take a vote.

B: Great idea.

30W: I agree.

B: Let's do it.

C: But I know the results.

M: (Looking at I) You don't make decisions like that. (Looking at C) You are pushing Toby toward the results you want. I am not.

D: You have. You are. Any fool can see that.

B: He has not.

CF: You're crazy.

B: (defiantly, like just before a fight) What?

LL: You're so blind.

I: C'mon. Let's vote or are you afraid of the outcome? You will be wrong.

B: Risk it, c'mon, risk it.

D: (shouting) You can't take that kind of a risk when you know a life is at stake.

TB: (shouts) Shut up!!! (they ignore him)

C: There is no risk if you know what someone truly wants!

M: But we don't.

    C: We do!

        D: (more firmly) We don't!

            I: We do!

    M: We most certainly do not!

        B: (mockingly) We most certainly do!

TB: Shut up! Stop it.(He continues this litany of "stop it, stop it...," shaking his head as though he can shake the voices out while he sticks his fingers in his ears. **As long as he keeps his fingers in his ears the voices stop though the mouths are moving, but when he takes them out the voices begin again at the former pitch.**)

D: How can you say you know what anyone wants you smart-mouthed little…

    B: Because I do…and you do

        LL: How can you say we do when we say we don't.

C: Because he knows that all of you who say "we don't' are like Toby earlier. He said he didn't know, but he did. Who wants to get it over with right now?

    CF: I can't believe how arrogant you are. You act so omniscient.

C: I don't have to be omniscient. (slowing down) It's all there in the life of Toby. (full of gestures and descriptive actions) Look at him when he takes his (says almost mockingly, with a quick hand motion) ritual bath. Look at him when he tries to go asleep. Look at how he tries to go asleep.

Look at him as he paces around in his apartment.
Look at him as he peeks out his windows. (Looking
at CF and then all around as he sleeps.) I act omniscient? I sense pain and agony. I also sense a
growing resolve. I know what he wants and you do
too if you have eyes. You don't need to be omniscient to hear Toby and know what he wants.

TB: (A loud, final whisper) STOP IT! I'm the one who
has to decide!(Everybody stops except C who moves
just a step toward TB.)

C: (looking from side to side) Are you ready to
act?

M: He said decide.

C: (his body language, smile, and nod show that he
accepts the challenge) Are you ready to (emphasizes
the word) decide?

TB: I can't stand it anymore. The life you've
described..., uh, that I've described...

LL: But that's not the only way to...

TB: (waves her off and moans to show his displea-
sure and to communicate his intention of finishing
his speech)...is too accurate. I'm sick of it. I'm
tired of this senate of voices which incessantly
argues inside of me. The last voice always seems
the most reasonable, the most compassionate, the
most feasible. And then another voice speaks up. I
can't stand any of it anymore. I'm going to...

CF: (quickly, but gently, knowing that TB is ever
so weak) Hey, buddy.(moves to TB's side) I
promise, I promise I'm going to let you finish,
but I have just a couple of things to say. You're
tired...

TB: I've heard this before.

CF: and wound up. Why not take a warm bath.(nods toward bathroom) You can think about what you want to do there.

C: (to CF) What a clever trick, but it won't work. Trying to get the boy's old sexual juices roll- ing. (he nods to the tub) Get him in the tub for a one-two then to bed, and tomorrow he's back on the job. (with confidence) You know, once you've slid on the ice, you never drive with the same confidence. In fact, you usually just pull to the side of the road, shaking and hoping to never drive again. Toby has been sliding for a long while and he doesn't need to drive anymore, doesn't want to.

CF: (Ignores C) What do you say? Run some water and go soak.

TB: I don't know.(Sits on the coffee table and stays there for a few moments. Then he speaks with a slight laugh) I do like my baths. (thinks) Maybe I will take a quick bath. Then I'll finish this matter.

[END OF THE SECOND MOVEMENT]

(Toby gets up slowly from the couch and crosses to the bathroom slowly unbuttoning his shirt as he goes. As he does this, the lights dim and some music, e.g. Led Zeppelin's KASHMIR, with a driving, slowly rhythmic beat begins. When he finishes his shirt, he slides on the bench which is serving as the bathtub. He pushes his pants down and puts his hand on his stomach, just above his underwear. All the characters pair up and begin to dance erotical- ly. C stands up on the coffee table with I and they observe this scene; he is the only one who remains motionless. D and M are, of course paired. B and LL perform the most erotically for she at first rejects him, but he woos her. When she gives in, she surrenders completely. CF and 30W dance the closest to TB; CF almost directs 30W in the move ments she makes. From time to time, 30W will step up on the bench with Toby so that he can touch her. The dialogue from this section is recorded so that the actors and actresses can have greater freedom. It should be recorded quicker then normal dialogue, but not so quick that it runs together. One might experiment with the reverb or echo for greater effect. **Or,** if the characters can say their lines while in the midst of their erotic "dance," that works. For TB to narrate his fantasy would help see his mounting excitement.)

TB: Why didn't I think of this sooner? Why didn't I do this sooner?

CF: (Looks at 30W and smiles slightly) Yeah, I bet it feels great. Just enjoy it, man.

C: (Looks at Toby, looks around at the others, looks at the small room, and let's his eyes rest on the open door. He speaks almost humorously, almost sarcastically, almost vindictively.) Toby, you should have shut the door; the gorilla might come and get you.

CF: Can't you leave him alone. (C shrugs his shoulders and leans against the sink on the other side of the room. CF turns his glance downward toward Toby)

TB: Boy, I'd like to see Mrs. Vickers right now. What a beautiful woman.

CF: (like a hypnotist—mind and mesmerizing) Call her up. You can see her. Call up your memories. Bring her to you.

TB: (as though he heard nothing) What a beautiful woman. I can still see her leaning over. Those breasts. Those thighs. I wanted to.. I want to...

B: Well, he's horny again.

CF: (to B) Cut it out; this is his special time.

B: You piss me off! First, we have to let him tell his stories, now we have to let him have his special time. I wish you would just go and...

CF: Don't listen to him, Toby. Go ahead.

TB: I go over to John's house and she, Mrs. Vickers, answers the door. She sees that I am sweaty and hot...

B: (over his shoulder) You can say that again.

TB: ...and she invites me in. I ask for John and she tells me that he was gone for the afternoon. She comments on how hot I look and offers me some lemonade. I hesitate at first, but then say that I really could use some. She tells me that she was thirsty too. She says that she has been out working in the backyard, in the garden. But I know that, for she is wearing my favorite outfit, that halter top and short shorts. (he slips his hand in his underwear and begins to manipulate himself) I follow her into the kitchen where she checks the refrigerator and finds out she needs to make more lemonade. I would try to leave, but she would keep me from leaving. She goes to the low cabinet where she keeps the lemonade mix. When she bends over, she does not squat, she leans over and her shorts pull up so that the bottom of her ass begins to show. She turns and says she only has fruit punch. Her halter gapes and her breasts hang. The way she turns the strap falls off her shoulder and I see her nipple. I feel her looking at me; I see her smile slightly. She knows what I'm thinking.

CF: (quietly) Good, good, Toby. Good story. It's working.

TB: (Toby looks down, shifts around and sighs. It is obvious that he is masturbating as he tells the

story.) I say fruit punch is okay so she takes that
package. She goes to the sink and begins to mix it.
I want her. I look at her back, bare except for a
strap and her shorts barely wedged in her crack.
Her hips are so full and her legs so long. (As he
says this line, 30W gets up on the bench with Toby
and he pushes one hand up her skirt. He rubs her
thigh as he rubs himself.) As the water nears the
top of the pitcher, I get up, quickly walk
behind her, and place my hands on her shoulders.
She looks up and out the window just over the sink
as she quickly turns the water off. She waits. My
hands slide down(he increases his manipulation) to
the clip on the back of her halter-top and I un-
clasp it. She has to set the pitcher in the sink
and bring her arms down on the front of her top so
that it doesn't fall off. She turns to look at me.
Then she let's go and the top falls to the floor.
She reaches out and pulls me to her. She begins to
kiss me. Between kisses, she begins to unbutton my
shirt. She pushes my shirt over my shoulders and it
falls to the floor. I kiss her and feel her breasts,
her nipples (the next three lines are said as he
says the following) are firm and I rub them and suck
on them and lick them...(Toby increases the tempo).

CF: (quietly) Good, good. Keep going. You're near
the peak.

TB: (almost shouting because he is so excited) She
steps back and unsnaps her shorts and tugs them and
her panties, in short back-and-forth, up-and-down
motions, until they fall off from their own weight.
She reaches over and feels the bulge in my pants.
As she moans, (30W begins to moan) she begins to
take off my jeans. She unsnaps them, pushes the
zipper down, and they fall to the floor. She drops
to her knees, pulls down my underwear, then takes
my hands to pull me on top of her. She keeps saying: **(30W): I want you, I want you, I've always
wanted you...inside of me.** I start to stick...

M: (The music abruptly **stops** and the recorded dialogue ends **when** M actually interrupts T's masturbation in a shamed, unbelieving, judgmental, repulsed tone.) Stop it! (Toby jerks his hand out of his underwear.) How vulgar! How disgusting! You should be ashamed that you have thoughts like that, that you do that!

CF: (surprised but also concerned for he knows the effect of interruptions) What? Shut up!

M: What has happened to decency? (Toby places his hand over his underwear to hide his erection.)

CF: Shut up! (CF looks down at TB's crotch.) Oh, no. But we can get back on track. Don't worry.

TB: (He is breathing heavily from M's attack and from the excitement.) I can't. I can't remember where I was.

CF: She had pulled you on the floor and wanted you inside of her.

30W: (Suddenly acting all righteous when she is really angry for his use of her.) What you men do to us! Get out of that tub, you bastard, and go meet a real woman. Don't sit in your tub with your hand on your prick, screwing make-believe, mind-less, mechanical puppets.

M: (in her own way agreeing) It's not right to think this way. It's not good to do this, this... (pointing down at Toby and further at his hand at his crotch then turning her head). It's not natural.

B: It is natural!

30W: I still say get a real date!

CF: Aw, shut up!(to them)(to Toby) Don't mind them.

Keep going, I'll deal with them.

30W: (Grabbing her crotch) You just better keep him out of here!

CF: (begins toward her and she waves him off and moves away)

TB: It's going down; I'm losing it. Where was I?

B: (leaning over) Lost it, huh?

CF: Leave him alone.(to Toby, beginning to get scared) C'mon Toby.

B: C'mon Toby. Read the recipe. Two parts tits, one part pussy. Add one firm dick. Blend imaginatively.

CF: Quit it!. C'mon Toby, she was pulling you down.

M; I can't believe this goes on and on.

B: (Looks over in the tub) It ain't going to go on very long.

TB: I can't get back. (looks down) God Damn **it**! I'm limp. (pause and then very forcefully) A guy that can't beat off is pathetic. (begins to cry)

C: (waits and allows the silence to accumulate. He looks around. He firmly, yet gently speaks.) Toby?!?!?!? Get dressed and come in here. (Toby dresses like a zombie while the others assemble, C watches Toby and directs the others with general motions to stand around him. CF, feeling defeated cowers at the back of the stage. Toby comes to the coffee table and sits there slouched over, his hands clasped in front of his body. The bag is lying on the table beside him. He pulls out the gun and a box of shells. He puts the shells on the coffee table; the gun hangs limp in his hand. He is staring straight out before him. C looks where

TB is looking for a long while and drops his eyes to the gun. He looks around at everyone, then down at the gun, then straight ahead.)

C: I see our role as helpers. We all know what you must do and we will help you do it.

D: (not as demonstrative, but firm—like a recruit who stands at attention but still speaks his mind) That's not my role. My role is to turn Toby around. He's made a bad decision and I'm not going to help him act on it.

C: I think it is clear that Toby feels strongly. You're wrong to put obstacles in his way.

M: You're wrong to push him.

C: (firmly) How many times do I need to tell you, I am not pushing him. I thought we cleared that up long ago.(sarcastically) Besides, why are you so concerned; you seem pretty repulsed in the bathroom there. That's Toby, that's what he does. That's life for Toby. When Toby is out of his misery, that "filth" will be gone.

M: How can I talk to you? Why do I try? You're heartless!

C: I'm right.

D: Right? You call believing a boy who is depressed...

C: Boy? Hold it! This is a twenty-nine-year old man.(briskly) We don't need to delay any longer. I want to see a show of hands of those who are prepared to let Toby go his own way.

(Throughout this subsequent discussion the characters once again ignore TB; they argue with each other. Before, they spoke to him, now they speak about him)

LL: Wait a minute.

    D: Certainly, wait a minute!

      CF: It never hurts to talk.

    M: You're pushing him over the brink.

      B: You're pushing me over the brink.

        D: I'd watch what I say.

      I: Let's not waste any more time. If he wants to...

LL: We must show him that he's wrong about himself.

    M: We have to try to give him hope.

C: And you say I push him. You want to put words in his mouth, thoughts in his head. You're the one who wants to run him.

    M: Because he is out of control. No person!

C: (says each word distinctly) That's your opinion.

    D: That's the truth.

        B: Says who?

    I: Everybody's opinion is just an opinion.

    D: Let's try to get...

TB: Hold it.

D:...some order...

TB: (quietly at first) Hold it. I want to see the vote.

30W: I'm not in favor of suicide, but he did say that he wanted to kill himself.

M: But he's not himself.

C: (loudly and abruptly) Well, then who is he?

D: You know what she means.

LL: We're just getting each other mad. If we will just slow down.

B: I say we let him go.

TB: (a bit more firmly) I want to see the vote.

I: I agree.

LL: How can you agree? This is a human life.

C: Toby is speaking to us.

LL: A human life.

I: Toby said what he wanted.

M: We must help him see that...

TB: (shouting) I want to see the vote! NOW!

C: (emphasizing his words) If HE wants to see the VOTE RIGHT NOW, I think we should show it to him.

M: But...

C: (raises his hand) HE SAYS HE WANTS TO SEE THE VOTE NOW!(short pause) All those in favor of stopping Toby, raise your right hand.(M, D, CF, and LL raise their hands. He does not vote.) One, two, three, four. Now all those in favor of Toby doing WHAT TOBY WANTS TO DO, raise your hands. (C, 30W, B and I raise their hands) one, two, three, four (looks down and Toby slowly lifts his hand), five! And the fifth vote is the most crucial.

M: Wait a minute, it's a tie because we're voting for him. He doesn't count.

C: (sharply) He's the only one who counts, he's always been the most important.

D: But you see how close it is. No one should be condemned on such a close vote.

C: We are not condemning him; we are allowing him to do what he wants.

I: This is crazy. He CAN do what he wants whether we let him or not.

M: But he really doesn't want to take his own life.

I: How can you say that? Did you see his arm, it was up. IT WAS UP!

C: (steps in) And how dare you continue to ignore the decision of Toby. He made a decision long ago. Some of us have officially recognized it. I believe we should let him proceed.

M: (emotionally moving toward a helpless frenzy—she separates from the crowd backing toward the bathtub) How can any of you stand here and let...

I: (firmly and slowly) It's what he wants.

M; But... (continues backing)

I: Lady, drop it. Toby wants it.

M: You just can't believe that.

30W: I believe it now. I wasn't sure. And he voted for it. (defensively) He has been talking about it for some time.

I: I agree with Toby; there's no other way out. Let him go.

M: I just can't let him go.

C: You've got a problem then, because Toby wants to go.

M: He does not.

LL: I agree with her (she moves toward M): he still has so much to offer.

D: Of course he still has so much to offer.

C: (angrily—he steps down and moves around the others always ending his lines looking at TB) I don't' know where you get these ideas. Toby has nothing to offer; he said so himself. Toby is tired of living, he said so himself. Toby has got a gun on the coffee table, he said so himself. See it? You can see that; can't you! Toby has voted for suicide, he did that himself. Listen to him. Listen to the rest of us who have listened to him. AND QUIT LISTENING TO YOUR FOOLISH IDEAS. YOU SAY HE WANTS TO LIVE; HE DOESN'T.

D: (moves around in front of TB and toward LL and M at the same time) Toby, surely, you, you had, really don't want to throw away your life by...

TB: (very deliberately) I want to do what I want to do. (reaches for the gun) And I'm going to use this on myself. (there are gasps from those who are so against his suicide. He picks up the gun, loads it, looks at the gun. The pro's move up close to him and C, the con's cluster with imploring looks on their faces but they are quiet because their arguments are futile)

C: (looking at the con's) (quietly) There.

TB: (TB places the gun several times to his temple testing the aim, the feel of the gun, the pressure of the gun against the temple. He laughs nervously.) I haven't done this too often so I'm kinda an amateur. And I want to do it right.

CF: (sarcastically, trying negative psychology, he moves around the group toward T) Yeah, you don't want to screw this up like everything else you've done.

TB: Damn you! Just shut up!

CF: I mean you've heard of the guy who blew the top part of his brain off and was a vegetable the rest of his life, that is, I think he died, but I may be wrong. Maybe he's still in the coma.

C and TB: Shut up. He's (I'm) going to get it right. (C smiles)

I: (sing-song) He does have a point. Get it right, Toby.

C: (put-out) He's going to get it right. (Looks at Toby)

I: (as though he's giving helpful information) Maybe if he stuck it in his mouth.

C: (squats down behind TB; speaks like a gun burst) No. (to Toby) Slant the gun, once you get it to your temple, slightly up and to the back. You did well to buy the bullets that explode. You will feel no pain, it will be quick. (TB practices that aim, then puts the gun in his lap. He is nervous, he is sweating, his hand is shaking slightly. He rubs his hands.) Toby, don't worry, that's natural, to be nervous. But you will get steady as you get closer to pulling the trigger. You will, I promise you.

M: (muffled and frenzied) He's manipulating him, hypnotizing him. (The cons embrace her.)

C: Don't rush: take your time.

TB: (He looks at the gun and wipes his forehead. He looks slowly around at the apartment and then looks down at the gun. He takes a deep breath, wipes his hands, and picks up the gun. He takes another deep breath and closes his eyes. He raises the gun to his temple and shifts it around. He blows out his breath loudly, takes in a breath, and grits his teeth.) (**Suddenly**, there is a loud knocking. TB screams as his arm reflexively jerks up and the gun fires. He throws the gun in front of him. He sits there feeling himself, moaning and breathing quickly and trying to figure out what happened. The knock comes again. Toby gets up, rushes to the door, angry with fear, opens the door and shouts.) What the hell do you want? (the postman, confused, surprised)

PM: What the hell is going on in there? I thought I heard a shot.

TB: (catching his breath and acting calm) Yeah, sure, everything's all right. I was loading a gun I bought for protection and when you knocked you almost scared me to death. The gun accidentally went off; I must have pulled the trigger.

PM: You're real lucky son. You made a hell of a hole in the ceiling. If you would have hit yourself, you would have done major damage.

T: I guess you're right. What do you want? My mail-box's downstairs.

PM: (motioning with his head toward the door) You have a large package...

T: (notices the package at the door) That's for me?

PM: Yeah. You have to have to sign for it. I'm glad you were here; I hate coming back when there's no one home. I'm sorry I gave you such a start. Now I don't need to lug this package back down to the truck, you know, and back to the post office. It's real heavy.

TB: (pushes PM out the door) Thank you. (The post-man leaves and TB pulls and pushes the large package into the living room in the front of the coffee table. He looks at the gun beside the pack-age.) God, he scared me. (thoughtful pause) Another couple of seconds and nobody could have scared me.

CL: That's right. Now, get it over with.

TB: Maybe I should check and see who the package is from.

C: Why? What does it matter? What does it **really** matter? Failures, jobs, shabby apartments, packag-es—they're all behind you.

TB: But I'm curious.

CF: Curiosity killed the cat.

C: (slowly like a teacher correcting a student.) Curiosity is not bad, it has its place and time. This is not the time or place.

TB: What does it matter? Why can't I find out who sent this (leans closer). Mom! Mom? What could she be sending me?

C: (stretches the name out for he is just a little bit peeved) Toby. Why do you torture yourself? This package has nothing in it that will change your life. It's not worth the time to check on. Don't waste any more time.

CF: Hey, Toby, maybe it's Pandora's box and all sorts of troubles will fly out at you. Gee, you might get hurt.

TB: Cut it out. You don't have to be so sarcastic.

C: That's the way Toby. Clear the way.

TB: But I don't think it is going to hurt to see what's in this package. I can do it when I'm ready.

M: Let him do what he wants.

C: I'm just trying to save you some trouble, some grief.

LL: Hah!

TB: I'm at least going to read this letter. (He tears off a letter that has been taped on the top of the package. He rips it open and unfolds a short letter. He begins to read and M's voice is heard:

***M: (acts as though she is writing the letter) Dear Son—You know how many times your father and I have said we were going to clean our house. I don't mean vacuum it, but really clean out the stuff we did not need anymore. We finally did it. We went through each room just piling everything in the floor we didn't need. We still kept too much. When we got to the hall closet, we hit a snag. It was just filled with your stuff, stuff you said you were going to take away someday, but you never have. So, we packed it up and sent it to you. Lots of stuff here,

annuals from junior high, high school, a fold-
er of your grade school stuff, a secret decoder, a
couple of letters you wrote to us while you were in
college, a few pictures of grade school friends, a
small bottle filled with your baby teeth. There's
even a picture of that goofy kid from junior high
you ran around with. Here it all is, enjoy the
memories. And most of all, enjoy all this junk that
you'll clean out in 30 or 40 years. Love, Mom.***

C: You see, Toby, you're right in line. It is
clean-up time.

B: They're clearing you out of their lives.

M: (Looks at C) They are not clearing him out, they
are sending him his memories. I don't know how you
can get your perverted ideas. You twist the facts.

C: We're beyond this bickering. (to TB) Now you
know what's in the box. It's time for you to do
your clean-up. C'mon.

TB: I would like to see what's actually there. It
won't take long.

C: Moving across the box from TB) Toby, look,
you've wasted enough time. I thought you had
learned your lesson, finally learned your lesson in
the tub. Nothing is going to make you feel better
except doing what you know you have to do. All the
diversions in the world are just that, diversions.
Opening this package will be just one more detour
that slams into a dead end. Stop the fantasy. Don't
waste any more time.

D: (righteously) By the same token, since he's now
on borrowed time, he might as well fill his mind
with memories.

C: The memories and thoughts which depress him?
The memories of his failures.

LL: For goodness sakes, there must be a few good memories there. Maybe he can fill his mind with those as he let's go.

D: Go ahead, Toby, if you want to open it. Do what YOU want to do.

TB: I am curious...and I don't think it will do any harm. (He begins to rip into the package. As he does all the others look interested, except B, I, 30W and C.)

C: This is just a stupid waste of time.

D: It's what he wants to do. This is more of his storytelling, you know "before he commits the act." We put up with it earlier, surely we can put up with it now.

C: (He is uneasy, something seems to be true about that reason, but something seems wrong, too.) I think this is a mistake.

D: Well, you can't argue with him doing what he wants to do. You argued for that earlier...

C: Oh shut up. (sing-song) Go on with your little excursion, Toby, but you're just...

M: (firmly but sarcastically) ...wasting time?

C: Well, it's true.

TB: What is this? Oh, no,(laughs) its my secret decoder. And a message. I wonder what it says. (he spells it out) T H E E N E M Y I S N E A R. (now says it) The enemy is near. B E W A R E. H E L P I S O N T H E W A Y (now says it) Beware, help is on the way. (again) R U B B E R M A N Rubber man. (he looks around as though he is playing, looks behind the couch, gets up and goes to the bathroom where he checks behind the door. Guess to the

78

window. Then, he says in an affected voice...) I
hope he makes it soon. I can't survive too long
without Rubberman. (laughs) (C looks off angrily,
shakes his head, starts to speak but stops) (TB
puts the box down, suddenly caught in a wave of
melancholy.) I haven't seen John, er, Rubberman,
in 14 years, ever since he moved away. That was a
lifetime ago. A short, unhappy lifetime.

C: (brightens up) Now you're coming to your
senses.

TB: Don't worry. I'm just going to glance at one
of these annuals and then I'll be through. (tosses
them aside, one by one, but quickly) Maybe my
senior year in high school. Look at this mush.
Dear Toby—you are a great guy and you will go far
in life. May God bless you and keep you. Love Linda
Kirby (John 3:16). Toby—Didn't we have the neatest
times in math analysis. Have a great life and stay
in touch. Eddie Jackson.

C: (squatting down) You know Toby, you're only
making yourself suffer. There aren't any good
memories here to carry with you. Even your good
memories have suffered. Trust me. When you really
look at your life, you can't be naïve any longer.
Be proud that you're not naïve. And quit torturing
yourself.

TB: Yeah, yeah, yeah. Give me a little time. I'm
saying good bye. I got nobody else right now and I
do feel like saying good bye.

C: Okay, but...(standing back up)

TB: I know, I know. (flips to the back cover). Hey,
Toby—This old high school will never be the same
without us super-high achievers will it? Hershel
(He momentarily slams the book shut, but swings it
open one more time and turns one page back) There's
only one on this page. (Looks at the bottom of the

page) Oh my God, I haven't thought of Cathy Phillips in years. She dated my best friend, but I really had a crush on her. (Pause)

LL: Toby! How do I write something that is not trite, something that you'll know I really mean. I guess I'll just write what I feel for you, my friend. You do not know how much you mean to me; we don't ever get a chance to talk about that. But you are my constant. I don't know how many times I came to chemistry feeling low. I would walk in, throw my books down on the desk, slump in my chair and listen to the chatter of our classmates. You would punch me and ask if I'd gotten rejected for the Captain Kangaroo show again. You didn't let me stay depressed. You joked, sure, but you always asked about me. Then, when you seemed so serious you would kid me again. I never left chemistry sad; I always left feeling good about myself. That was your gift to me and I will never forget that gift. And I will never forget you. Love, Cathy**

(TB wipes his eyes and looks around the room. He begins to cry. He gets up and walks around, finally going to the couch to sit down. (**Toby resumes**) I will never forget you. I wonder if she would find it so hard to forget me now? (he let's the book ease to the floor under the coffee table) About to blow out my brains.

C: Toby. Cut it out. Shut the book. You've done enough reflecting. Cathy and all those people lie back there, they're not with you now. They can't help you; (pause) they didn't help you. Let them go.

LL: Cathy didn't let you go. (moving to the coffee table)

C and TB: What do you mean?

LL: I don't mean you two didn't go your separate

ways. You did, but a part of you stayed with her and changed her and helped her. I know it.

C: I despise sentimentality.

TB: (smiling slightly, dreamily) She said I had a gift to cheer her up, to help her see the good in her. When did I lose that gift?

D: Maybe when you began expecting the world to hand you what you wanted.

C: (Quick and angry) What does that mean? "When you began expecting the world to hand you what you wanted." Nonsense! (laughs) Nonsense.

D: No, I mean when you began expecting everybody to fit your pattern. You went to school, to college, and expected to walk out and someone to pick you up and plug you in. You no longer relied upon your-self; you relied too much on your expectations, on your picture of the world.

C: How long do we have to endure this amateur psychological analysis?

   B: Does seem like a lecture from the school counselor.

      I: (to D) What's the point?

D: The point is that he,... he began to trip up, he become more and more unsure of himself.

B: (angrily) Cut this out!. It doesn't take a genius to see that his guy is washed up. No matter how you explain it, he is through.

M: It does make a difference.

      B: Why?

D: Because the way you tell a story is part of the story, and its conclusion.

B: What?

D: The way you tell the story determines how it ends.

C: Riddles! Useless riddles! Toby!

TB: You mean the way you see yourself changes the story?

LL: Yes, you can see yourself differently.

C: They are wrong, wrong! The way you are is your story. You have rightly seen your life and you have rightly told your story. You have decided to write the final chapter because you realized that the main character could not be developed any further. This nonsense of theirs is worse than death. Toby, quit bothering with these, with these...

LL: With these people who know you and love you, like Cathy. Your life has been sabotaged by your fear and your blindness. It's as though someone, or something, maybe your expectations, or life, hit you and you lost your way, you began to live in fear. That person who Cathy knew is still right here.

C: Toby!

TB: (Interested, to C) It's not going to hurt to take a little more...

B: What a coward! First your stories, you told your abominable stories for God knows how long so you wouldn't have to admit that you wanted to kill yourself.

I: Then you finally admitted that you wanted to kill

yourself.

LL: (angrily digging in for the last struggle) I've
felt deeply all along that those stories were a
sign of the will to live, not the desire to die.

M: (strongly) Of course they were.

B: No. No. All we are seeing now is another sign of
his willy-nilly mind, and his gutless life.

I: (To TB) Coward! (To the others) Anybody can see
that he's backing out, he's slinking back into the
"old routine." Sliding back. Putting it off.(mocking) I know you mean well, but you don't have what
it takes.

B: That's right. Listen to the way you talk. You
weren't and you were, then you can and you can't.
You know and you don't know. You're confused, you
see clearly, you're up, you're down, you're out,
you're in.(makes his judgement) you're totally
screwed and tattooed. You made a careful, considered decision. I'm tired of all of this stalling
and I say go with the majority and the majority
said: "Do it!" And you did too!

D: Wait a minute. It does not just take courage to
die at your own hand, it takes courage to live. I
would add, it takes much more courage to live with
all that life throws at you.

M: It takes a great deal of courage to face up to
people misled, to decisions spoiled, to years
wasted or to possibilities denied. It takes a
courage that almost leads to despair but ultimately
gets to the other side of the valley.

C: Oh, Toby, boy. Listen to me. Shut all these
voices out. Don't let this moment of longing for
what you've never had and never will have lead you
astray, don't let these sentimental voices keep you

from the truth you have embraced.(Looks at D) Don't let them keep you from your moment of pure courage. Pick up the gun.

M: Don't let him keep you from an act of courage, choose life. Face life...risk trying again.

C: Damn it, Toby, pick up the gun. Do it. NOW!

CF: (softly) Listen to my voice; don't.

I: Take the gun, you chicken.

B: Come on, shoot your head off.

LL: No. No.

D: You mustn't. Listen to me.

I: Take the gun. That's the only sensible thing to do. You've made plans.

30W: Go ahead.

LL: Don't listen to them.

B: Don't listen to her.

D: Get up Toby. Get away from the gun.

C: (enraged, commanding) Toby!

LL: Please, please. Listen to those who...

TB: (he walks briskly to the gun and looks down at it) Stop it! (the whole group freezes, each one mirroring their own conclusions as to what this means) (TB start to lean down to get the gun but stands back up and kicks the gun as he utters a shriek from deep in his gut) Ohwuhhhhhh! (He stands breathing heavily his head bowed and his arms hanging limply at his side.)

C: Why did you do that? (he waits, then truly curious asks a question) What are you going to do now?

TB: (He goes to the box, throws the stuff back in the box, runs over, gets his jacket by the door, comes back to box, but keeps looking around) Where is that?

C: Where is what? The gun's over there where you kicked it.

TB: (keeps looking) No, not that. (pause) There it is. (he sees the annual and he retrieves it)

C: What are you doing?

TB: I'm leaving.

C: How can you leave? Where can you go? (hesitates) Wait until the morning. Think about this. Get some rest and think about it.

TB: No, I've wasted enough time. I ought to go right now. I don't really need very much. All I need is these clothes...and me...(he moves quickly across the room with the annual) And, my gift. (He picks up the box and moves quickly to the door but stops when C speaks.)

C: (desperate and incredulous) How can you go when just a few moments ago you finally realized how desperate you were. How meaningless your life really was? How can you leave and put off again what you need to do. How can you deny the truth? What makes you think that a split-second of nostalgia and a couple of laughs can change your life?

TB: I can't really explain it, but I was jolted by life. I had this idea that it just unfolded and you went along. But when my expectations exploded, I got knocked down, trampled on, and blinded. When you can't see, you become even more afraid. The unknown becomes infinite. I was knocked around some more today, but sometime, well, when I was reading what Cathy said, it was like a tremendous blow to my head, but then my head was filled with warmth. All of a sudden instead of being in a dark cave I came into the light. I know I'm not going to like everything I see, the world is not all beautiful. I'll have to work hard; I'll need to make up for time lost. My life's not a pretty sight, but I can see again. I can see what i might be, what it might become and that's hopeful, hope-filled. (opens the door)

C: Toby, you can't run away, we'll be with you.

TB: I know. I'm not afraid. (Goes through and shuts the door. The stage immediately goes dark.)